Harvard Business Review

ON

MANAGING YOUR CAREER

IN TOUGH TIMES

THE HARVARD BUSINESS REVIEW PAPERBACK SERIES

The series is designed to bring today's managers and professionals the fundamental information they need to stay competitive in a fast-moving world. From the preeminent thinkers whose work has defined an entire field to the rising stars who will redefine the way we think about business, here are the leading minds and landmark ideas that have established the *Harvard Business Review* as required reading for ambitious businesspeople in organizations around the globe.

Other books in the series:

Other books in the series (continued):

Harvard Business Review

ON

MANAGING YOUR CAREER
IN TOUGH TIMES

A HARVARD BUSINESS REVIEW PAPERBACK

Library of Congress Cataloging-in-Publication Data

Harvard Business review on managing your career in tough times.
        p. cm. — (A Harvard Business review paperback) Includes
index.
    ISBN 978-1-4221-3343-9 (pbk.)
  1. Career development.   2. Job security.   3. Career changes.
4. Vocational guidance.   I. Harvard Business School. Press.
II. Harvard business review.
    HF5381.H279 2009
    650.1—dc22

                                                    2009030666

Table of Contents

Harvard Business Review

ON

MANAGING YOUR CAREER

IN TOUGH TIMES

How to Protect Your Job in a Recession

JANET BANKS AND DIANE COUTU

Executive Summary

AS THE ECONOMY SOFTENS, corporate down-sizing appears almost inevitable. Don't panic yet, though. While layoff decisions might seem beyond your control, there's plenty you can do to make sure you retain your job.

In this article, Banks, a former HR executive at Chase Manhattan and FleetBoston Financial, and Coutu, an HBR senior editor and former affiliate scholar at the Boston Psychoanalytic Society and Institute, describe how to improve your chances of survival. It's mostly a matter of coolheaded plann-ing, they observe. When cuts loom, the first thing to do is *act* like a survivor. Be confident and cheer-ful. Research shows that congeniality trumps com-petence when push comes to shove. Look to the

1

future by focusing on customers, for without them, no one will have work. Survivors also tend to be versatile; tight budgets demand managers who can wear several hats, so start demonstrating what other capabilities you can offer. If you're, say, a manager who once worked as a teacher, take on a training role.

Remember to be a good corporate citizen: Participation matters now more than ever. It isn't the time to behave as if work is beneath you or to argue for a new title. When one executive's department was folded under the management of a less-experienced colleague, she swallowed her pride and wholeheartedly supported the new hierarchy. Her superiors noticed her commitment and eventually rewarded her with a prestigious appointment.

It's also important to offer leaders hope and realistic solutions. Energize your colleagues around change, like the VP of learning at a firm undergoing major staff reductions did. He organized a humorous in-house radio show that revived spirits and helped management communicate with employees—and ended up with a promotion.

IN A TROUBLED ECONOMY, job eliminations and hiring freezes seem almost routine, but when your own company's woes start to make headlines, it all hits home. Intellectually, you understand that downsizing isn't personal; it's just a law of commerce, but your heart sinks at the prospect of losing your position. While you know that passivity is a mistake, it's hard to be proactive when your boss's door is always closed, new projects are put on hold, and your direct reports look to you for reassurance. Don't panic. Even though layoff decisions may be beyond your control, there's plenty you can do.

That's what we've observed in numerous layoffs over the years and in research on how people respond to stressful work conditions. (Author Janet Banks oversaw a dozen downsizings as a vice president in human resources at Chase Manhattan Bank and a managing director at FleetBoston Financial. Author Diane Coutu studied resilience during her time as an affiliate scholar at the Boston Psychoanalytic Society and Institute.) We've seen that while luck plays an important role, survival is most often the result of staring reality in the face and making concrete plans to shape the future. Machiavellian as it may seem, holding on to your job when the economy softens is a matter of cool strategic planning. In our experience, however, even the savviest executives are ill-prepared to deal with job threats. Here's what you can do to keep your career moving and minimize the chances that you'll become a casualty.

Act Like a Survivor

A popular partner in the Brussels office of McKinsey & Company mentored hosts of junior consultants. When asked for advice on getting ahead, he always gave the same reply: "If you want to be a partner, start acting like one." The corollary of this advice is even more important: During a recession, you have to start acting like a survivor if you hope to escape the ax.

Studying the thinking of survivors reveals a surprising paradox. Though creating a plan to weather layoffs requires an almost pessimistic realism, the best thing you can do in a recession is lighten up. Keep your eye firmly on the eight ball, but act confident and cheerful. Research shows that being fun to be around really matters. Work by Tiziana Casciaro and Miguel Sousa Lobo, published in a June 2005 HBR article, "Competent Jerks, Lovable Fools, and the Formation of Social Networks," shows that while everyone prefers working with a personable superstar to an incompetent jerk, when people need help getting a job done, they'll choose a congenial colleague over one who is more capable but less lovable. We're not suggesting that you morph into Jerry Seinfeld; being congenial and fun isn't about bringing down the house. Just don't be the guy who's always in a bad mood, reminding colleagues how vulnerable everyone is. Who wants to be in the trenches with him?

Of course, putting on a good face can be psychologically exhausting when rumors of downsizing spread. Change always stirs up fears of the unknown. Will you land another job? How will you pay the mortgage? Can you find affordable health insurance? Those are all valid concerns, but if you stay positive, you'll have more influence on how things play out.

Survivors are also forward looking. Studies of concentration camp victims show that people made it through by imagining a future for themselves. The power of focusing on the times ahead is evident even among people suffering the blows of everyday life. As Freud wrote in "Mourning and Melancholia," a critical difference between ordinary grief and acute depression is that mourners can successfully anticipate a life where there will once again be joy and meaning.

In your job, there's no better way to look forward than to stay focused on customers, for without them no one will have a job in the future. Anticipating the needs of your customers, both external and internal, should be your top priority. Prove your value to the firm by showing your relevance to the work at hand, which may have shifted since the economy softened. Your job is less likely to be eliminated if customers find that your contribution is indispensable.

Being ambidextrous will increase your chances of survival as well. In one company we know of, senior staff members were often expected to play more than one role to keep expenses in check. When the organization's new chief operating officer decided he needed a chief of staff, he chose a person who continued to manage a human resources team, thereby eliminating the need for additional head count. Reorganizations and consolidations involve great change, so they demand versatile executives. If you're not already wearing multiple hats, start imagining how you can support your company by leveraging experience your boss may know nothing about. A marketing manager who taught school before moving into industry might volunteer to take on sales and service training responsibilities, for example. A recession can offer you plenty of opportunities to display your capabilities. Layoffs typically occur at all levels of an organization and can create vacuums above and below you.

Finally, survivors are willing to swallow a little pride. Take the case of Anne, a manager at a large New England insurance company. (We've changed her name, as well as those of the other individuals cited in this article.) During a reorganization, Anne found herself vying for a position with a colleague who had far less industry experience than she did. When she learned that she and her department would be folded under this colleague's department, Anne realized that she had one choice if she

wanted to keep her job—use her significant influence to
support her new manager. So she publicly threw herself
behind the colleague. In turn, he gave her the respect and
the loyalty she felt she deserved. Anne's attitude demonstrated commitment to the company—something that
was noticed by the management. A year later Anne got
new responsibilities that led to a prestigious board
appointment.

Give Your Leaders Hope

It's important to recognize that times of uncertainty are
also tough for leaders. They don't enjoy having to lay off
their people; most find that task agonizing. It can be
stressful and time-consuming for them to sort through
the various change mandates they've been given and
then decide what to do. Obviously, this isn't the time to
push for a promotion or to argue for a new job title.
Instead, try to help the leader defend your department. If
the boss is working on a restructuring plan and asks for
ideas, offer some realistic solutions. Don't fight change;
energize your colleagues around it.

It may sound like what Karl Marx called *false
consciousness*—thinking that disempowers you because
it is not in your best interest—to empathize with your
boss when he or she is considering cutting your job.
However, there's science to support the idea that showing empathy for people more powerful than you can be
worthwhile. For example, recent mother-infant research
shows that the more an infant smiles and interacts with
the environment, the more active the caretaker becomes
in the infant's development and survival. Although the
mother-infant research has not, to our knowledge, been
replicated in the workplace, psychologists have shown

that so-called attachment behavior—emotional bonding—can be learned, just as emotional intelligence skills can be honed. That's good news. The better your relationship with your manager, the less likely you are to be cut, all things being equal. Your ability to empathize can demonstrate a maturity that is invaluable to the company, not least because it models good behavior for others.

The ability to unite and inspire colleagues goes a long way in the best of times; in the worst it's crucial. This was true at an international financial services company that had endured a staff reduction of 20%. In the face of low morale, the head of human resources asked Isaac, a learning and development VP, to help revive people's spirits, improve communications, and stir up some fun. Isaac quickly pulled together a small team of volunteers and created a live radio show that engaged even the most cynical members of the organization. It included a soap opera that kept staff at all levels laughing and waiting for the next episode. The show gave executives a unique platform to share information such as quarterly financial results and changes in the organization's structure. It did so much to improve morale that as a result Isaac landed the job he wanted—head of management and leadership development for the company.

Become a Corporate Citizen

Remember Woody Allen's remark that 80% of success is showing up? That is especially useful advice in a downturn. Start going to all those voluntary and informal meetings you used to skip. Be visible. Get out of your office and walk the floor to see how folks are doing. Take part in company outings; if the firm is gathering for the annual golf tournament and you can't tell a wood from an iron, then go along just for fun. In tough times, leaders look for employees who are enthusiastic participants. It's not the score that counts.

Corporate citizens are quick to get on board. Consider Linda, a VP in operations, who worked in a large company that needed to cut costs. Management came up with the idea of shared service centers to avoid duplication of effort in staff functions in areas such as compensation, management training, and strategic planning. The decision was universally unpopular. Service center jobs had none of the cachet of working in small business units, where customized solutions could be developed. Headquarters staff objected to losing the elite status they'd enjoyed as corporate experts. When service center jobs were posted, many high-profile people refused to put their names forward, misjudging their own importance and hoping management would relent. But Linda saw the opportunity and applied for a service center job. The new position gave her immense visibility and was an immediate promotion. Meanwhile, many of the resisters found themselves standing without a chair when the music stopped. In contrast, Linda kept her career on track; six years later she reported directly to the president of the company.

Of course, changing your behavior or personality to survive may rub against your need for authenticity, and you may decide that it's time to move on. In that case, you can be both true to yourself and the ultimate corporate citizen by volunteering to leave the organization. Despite what the policy may be, companies will cut deals. Deals are even welcomed. It's much less painful for managers if they can help someone out the door who wants to leave rather than give bad news to someone who depends on the job. If you're a couple of years away from retirement eligibility and want to go, ask the company if it would be willing to bridge the time. Float a few balloons, but don't get greedy. Keep in mind that even if you choose to go, you may need to get another job and you'll want good references and referrals. If you've exited gracefully, odds are, your boss and others will do whatever they can to help you land on your feet.

Many forces are beyond your control in a recession, but if you direct your energy toward developing a strategy, you'll have a better chance of riding out the storm. You have to be extremely competent to make it through, but your attitude, your willingness to help the boss get the job done, and your contribution as a corporate citizen have a big impact on whether you are asked to stick around. The economy will bounce back; your job is to make sure that you do, too.

Preparing for the Worst: You May Still Need a Plan B

Following the best advice is no guarantee that you won't get laid off. That's why you need a plan for handling a job loss.

The first key to moving on successfully is self-awareness. You'll have better luck finding a new job if you know what you're good at and what you'd really like to do, so it's wise to invest mental energy now in figuring those things out. If you have results from a Myers-Briggs test or a 360-degree assessment, revisit them to understand your strengths and weaknesses. Read self-help books to inspire your thinking, or perhaps even hire an executive coach. (Just make sure to get references and agree on fees before you start with any coach.)

Don't wait till you get laid off to update your résumé. Revise it now, so that you'll have it ready when you start approaching headhunters, former bosses and colleagues, and industry contacts for job referrals and advice. It's a good idea to begin networking with those folks now, in fact, but don't stop there. Reach out to the neighbor who's the CFO of a successful company, and dig out the old business cards from your drawer and add those names to the list of those you'll call.

Finally, think creatively about your future. Perhaps you want to go back to school, start your own business, join a smaller firm, or become a minister. That may require some downsizing of your own, but as Ellen, a consultant, told us: "Now that the kids are grown, my husband looks at the house and says it's too big for the two of us. I'm willing to scale back. Both of us want to do different things." Who knows, maybe plan B will actually be more attractive than plan A.

Originally published in September 2008
Reprint R0809J

Courage as a Skill

KATHLEEN K. REARDON

Executive Summary

A DIVISION VICE PRESIDENT blows the whistle on corruption at the highest levels of his company. A young manager refuses to work on her boss's pet project because she fears it will discredit the organization. A CEO urges his board, despite push back from powerful, hostile members, to invest in environmentally sustainable technology. What is behind such high-risk, often courageous acts?

Courage in business, the author has found, seldom resembles the heroic impulsiveness that sometimes surfaces in life-or-death situations. Rather, it is a special kind of calculated risk taking, learned and refined over time. Taking an intelligent gamble requires an understanding of what she calls the "courage calculation": six discrete decision-making processes that make success more likely while averting rash or unproductive behavior. These include setting attainable goals, tipping the power balance in your favor, weighing risks against benefits, and developing contingency plans.

Goals may be organizational or personal. Tania Modic had both types in mind when, as a young bank manager, she overstepped her role by traveling to New York—on vacation time and on her own money—to revitalize some accounts that her senior colleagues had allowed to languish. Her high-risk maneuver benefited the bank and gained her a promotion.

Lieutenant General Claudia J. Kennedy weighed the risks and benefits before deciding to report a fellow officer who had plagiarized a research paper at a professional army school. In her difficult courage calculation, loyalty to army standards proved stronger than the potential discomfort and embarrassment of "snitching" on a fellow officer.

When the skills behind courageous decision making align with a personal, organizational, or societal philosophy, managers are empowered to make bold moves that lead to success for their companies and their careers.

A DIVISION VICE PRESIDENT blows the whistle on corruption at the highest levels of his company. A young manager refuses to work on her boss's pet project because she fears it will discredit the organization. A CEO urges his board, despite push back from powerful, hostile members, to make a serious investment in environmentally sustainable technology. Such things happen every day in firms around the world. What is behind these high-risk, often courageous acts?

The U.S. senator and onetime prisoner of war John McCain has defined courage as a brief, singular occurrence: "that rare moment of unity between conscience, fear, and action, when something deep within us strikes the flint of love, of honor, of duty, to make the spark that fires our resolve." This definition conjures up an image of the lone hero who—instinctively, spontaneously, and against all odds—suddenly takes charge and stands up for virtue.

Certainly, courage is sometimes a matter of life and death. Police officers and firefighters risked and lost their lives saving people on September 11, 2001; people dove into swirling waters to rescue strangers after a giant tsunami swept Indonesia in 2004. Yet in my 25 years of studying human behavior in organizations, I've discovered that courage in business seldom operates like this. Through interviews with more than 200 senior and midlevel managers who have acted courageously—whether on behalf of society, their companies, their colleagues, or their own careers—I've learned that this kind of courage is rarely impulsive. Nor does it emerge from nowhere.

In business, courageous action is really a special kind of calculated risk taking. People who become good leaders have a greater than average willingness to make bold moves, but they strengthen their chances of success—and avoid career suicide—through careful deliberation and preparation. Business courage is not so much a visionary leader's inborn characteristic as a skill acquired through decision-making processes that improve with practice. In other words, most great business leaders teach themselves to make high-risk decisions. They learn to do this well over a period of time, often decades.

Learning to take an intelligent gamble requires an understanding of what I call the "courage calculation": a method of making success more likely while avoiding rash, unproductive, or irrational behavior. Six discrete processes make up the courage calculation: setting primary and secondary goals; determining the importance of achieving them; tipping the power balance in your favor; weighing risks against benefits; selecting the proper time for action; and developing contingency plans.

Setting Goals

The first component of the courage calculation answers these questions: What does success look like in this high-risk situation? Is it obtainable? If my primary goal is organizational, does it defend or advance my company's or team's principles and values? If my primary goal is personal, does it derive solely from my career ambitions or also from a desire for my organization's or even society's greater good? If I can't meet my primary goal, what is my secondary goal?

Suppose a well-regarded coworker is about to be fired. He has been maligned, and the person who poisoned his well did so to clear his own path to promotion. Colleagues have been grumbling about this, but no one has stepped forward to counter the false accusations. The senior manager who will do the firing is a poor listener and tends to kill messengers. Given the politics, should you try to save your coworker? Would doing so advance both the firm's and your own goals, preferably without making the senior manager look inept?

Whether primary or secondary, your goals should be reasonably within reach, not pie-in-the-sky ambitions. A primary goal that serves the organization might be either to rescue a good employee or to prevent the senior manager from acting on faulty information. A secondary organizational goal might be to apprise the senior manager of a "rat" in the company's midst. A primary goal that serves you personally might be to receive some behind-the-scenes credit for helping the employee. A secondary personal goal might be to feel that you did something for the greater good.

Although the odds of success will be hard to estimate before the other decisions in the courage calculation have been made, it is possible at this stage to think about the likelihood of primary-goal achievement. The venture capitalist Tania Modic, for instance, managing partner of Western Investments Capital, took a big risk in her first job out of college, as the assistant marketing development officer at an international bank. Modic's fancy title had a catch: There was no marketing development officer for her to assist, and the work she was assigned was unchallenging. The ambitious Modic wanted to contribute to the bank's success and also to her own advancement. Having helped many people senior to her, she knew she had the skills to do their jobs. So, using vacation time and her own money, she traveled to New York, called on some accounts that her senior colleagues had allowed to languish, and revitalized them. When she returned, some high-placed noses were out of joint, but her courageous action gained the attention of senior management, and she was rewarded with praise and, later, a promotion.

Modic was not merely brash. She thought clearly about her goals and the circumstances surrounding her high-risk maneuver: the culture of the organization, her personal history and skills, and the points of view of others involved. Her primary goal was organizational— to revitalize the dead accounts—and she estimated her chances of achieving that goal at about 70%. Her secondary goal was personal—to raise her visibility—and she saw a 60% chance of succeeding at that. She estimated her chances of getting fired at about 50%—or higher if she failed to rescue the accounts. Modic decided that she could live with these odds: The upside for the bank was considerable, and for herself, she believed, even bad visibility was better than none. She took the plunge, and went on to an impressive career. Like many effective leaders, Modic succeeded by recognizing, early in her career, the advantages of careful risk calculation over impulsiveness.

Determining Your Goals' Importance

The second component of the courage calculation addresses these questions: Just how important is it that you achieve your goal or goals? If you don't do something about the current state of affairs, will your company suffer? Will your career be derailed? Will you be able to look at yourself in the mirror? Does the situation call for immediate, high-profile action or something more nuanced and less risky? Courage is not about squandering political capital on low-priority issues.

To distinguish such squandering from constructive risk, John Hallenborg, a Los Angeles–based senior entertainment manager, assigns importance at three levels. On the lowest rung of his risk-taking ladder are issues about which he does not feel strongly, though he may prefer a particular outcome and may say so in a low-risk situation. Middle-rung issues are those about which his opinion is strong but doesn't involve higher values; his feelings may change based on new information. At the top of the ladder are "spear in the sand" issues. He perceives these as resting on morals or values for which he is willing to take a stand and fight.

Spear-in-the-sand situations require that you weigh your belief in the cause against the risks involved. Such situations are rare: They occur when negotiation is difficult or impossible, open minds are hard to find, and doing nothing is simply not an option. Peter Rost, a physician, formerly with Pfizer, drove his spear into the sand when he broke ranks with his employer by calling for legislation allowing the import of lower-priced medicines from Canada and elsewhere—a practice the U.S. drug industry strongly opposes. He also put his job on the line in efforts to halt the sale of off-label drugs and the associated incentives for physicians. Rost did not take on the pharmaceutical industry lightly, and the move cost him his career. But his convictions were too strong to ignore. He left the industry and went on to write *The Whistleblower: Confessions of a Healthcare Hitman.*

Tipping the Power Balance

People often assume that power in corporations is a simple matter of position on the organization chart. In attempting to please those above them, many people choose never to take a stand. But in reality, even those in top management give power to anyone on whom they are dependent—whether for respect, advice, friendship, appreciation, or network affiliations. Seen this way, power is something over which we really do have considerable control. By establishing relationships with and influencing those around you, for example, you gain sway over people who otherwise hold sway over you. This gives you a broader base from which to make bold moves.

You can wisely form supportive power networks in advance, but building them takes time. In 1981 Jack Gallaway developed his power base as part of a courage calculation on behalf of Ramada. At the time, Gallaway was president of the Tropicana hotel and casino in Las Vegas, which Ramada owned. The company, having spent $340 million to construct its Atlantic City casino, was selling off hotels to make up for a 300% cost overrun. The last thing Ramada's board and top managers wanted to consider was any kind of expansion. But Gallaway believed that expansion in the booming Las Vegas market was critical.

When he approached Ramada's senior managers about adding another hotel tower to the Tropicana, they told him to stick to his knitting. "They wouldn't even give me the money to work on the concept designs," he recalls. He decided to see what he could do by leveraging his external network: He contacted an executive with Mardian, a Phoenix-based real estate developer. This was a clever move, because the powerful chairman of Ramada himself had previously passed on the executive's name.

Gallaway knew that Mardian was in the process of building a stadium in Las Vegas, and that the executive and other employees would need a place to stay while in town. So he made a trade: He provided Mardian's people with hotel rooms and transportation for a week in exchange for a complete set of concept drawings and an architectural model of a new Tropicana tower, worth more than $100,000. Mardian's senior managers knew this would give them the inside track if the hotel expansion was actually undertaken.

Gallaway's calculation paid off. When the Atlantic City operation opened in 1982, Ramada was again in the black, and Gallaway made his move. He presented Ramada's board with the drawings and the model, and the board approved the project. He knew that he could have been handed his head for going against the board's instructions, but he lowered the risks by tipping the power balance—working with someone he'd found through Ramada's chairman. Meanwhile, he proved himself a loyal "citizen" by keeping his operation's numbers up. By the time the company's financial crisis was over, Gallaway had secured an invaluable foothold in Las Vegas.

Weighing Risks and Benefits

This component of the courage calculation focuses on trade-offs. Who stands to win? Who stands to lose? What are the chances that your reputation will be tarnished beyond repair if you go forward? Will you lose respect or your job? Cause others to lose theirs? Delay your opportunity for promotion?

Lieutenant General Claudia J. Kennedy, the first female three-star general in the U.S. Army, went through a difficult risk-benefit assessment before reporting a fellow officer who had plagiarized a research paper at a professional army school. Kennedy weighed the negatives (discomfort and embarrassment for "snitching" on a fellow officer) against the positives (allegiance to the army's high standards for its future leaders, and adherence to her own ethics). The decision was difficult: An instinct for self-protection, loyalty to her colleagues and to the institution, and her personal integrity all contended within her. She considered speaking privately to the officer, but realized that he would react angrily and that, after all, it wasn't her job to manage him. In the end, she decided that her loyalty to army standards was paramount: "I. . .recognized that overlooking an ethical lapse was tantamount to participating in the event," she writes in her book *Generally Speaking*. She discreetly reported the incident; her reputation remained intact and her career thrived.

Other trade-offs deal with the quality of the action and the strategy involved. Are your goals better served if you act in a direct and forceful way or if you take an indirect approach? A story I call "Send Him a Rose" exemplifies the calculation required here. A division vice president who had a habit of enraging underlings stormed into the office of Rick Sanders (not his real name), the editor of an in-house corporate newspaper. The VP accused Sanders of not having checked his facts before printing a story about the VP's division. He ranted and raved, giving Sanders no chance to point out that the facts in question had come from the VP's own assistant.

At first Sanders wanted to send the executive a scathing e-mail. He knew that doing so would mean saying good-bye to his job. He was angry enough not to care, but he considered the costs to his division: The VP would probably refuse to work with Sanders's colleagues in the future, and their reputation with the CEO would be sullied. Sanders was far less willing to chance this. "If I reacted too strongly," he remembers thinking, "I'd run a big risk of hurting my team. Still, I felt I had to do something."

Sanders chose a judolike approach suggested by a colleague, who told him to "send the VP a rose" in the form of a disarmingly professional memo. The memo reminded the executive of the good relations their two departments had enjoyed over the years. Sanders said he regretted the inaccuracy but mentioned that the facts had been checked with the VP's assistant. He ended with a hope for positive collaboration in the future. The memo was not apologetic; rather, it was civil and to the point, and it invited a higher level of discourse—in essence, teaching the executive how to behave like one. After calculating the benefits of such a move, Sanders opted for what John F. Kennedy, in *Profiles in Courage,* described as a less glorified but nevertheless critical form of courage, which achieves the better outcome through a willingness to replace conflict with cooperation.

A few weeks later, Sanders happened to see the vice president. Instead of glaring reproachfully at Sanders or ignoring him, the VP shook his hand respectfully and said, "It's a pleasure working with you." The memo, which demonstrated a level of professionalism the executive himself had failed to display, paid off. Whereas countless others had crashed on the VP's reef, Sanders preserved an important relationship for his division and for himself. He also learned that he could deal with a tough customer in a creative way.

Selecting the Right Time

Desmond Tutu has described good leaders as having an uncanny sense of timing. "The real leader," he writes, knows "when to make concessions, when to compromise, when to employ the art of losing the battle in order to win the war."

It can be argued that when someone is confronted by a situation that requires courage, the question of timing should be irrelevant. We assume that in spear-in-the-sand situations, when much is at stake and emotions are running high, brave people don't hesitate to act. This may be true in emergency situations, but a single-minded rush to action in business is usually foolish.

Consider what happened when one group of senior managers pressured their CEO, who was in his seventies, to produce a succession plan a year before he was ready to do so. The CEO, who had always treated his managers like family, was deeply hurt. Though he wasn't opposed to the notion of succession planning, he considered the forcing of it premature and impertinent. Had the managers waited, the CEO later told me, they would have accomplished their mission. But they were adamant. The CEO's anger grew; he edged out one manager, and the others were soon looking for new jobs.

Although emotion is always in the mix, and may even be an asset when making a courageous move, the following questions can help in logically calculating whether the time is right:

- Why am I pursuing this now?

- Am I contemplating a considered action or an impulsive one?

- How long would it take to become better prepared? Is that too long?

- What are the pros and cons of waiting a day, two days, a week or more?

- What are the political obstacles? Can these be either removed or reduced in the near future?

- Can I take steps now that will create a foundation for a courageous move later?

- Am I emotionally and mentally prepared to take this risk?

- Do I have the expertise, communication skills, track record, and credibility to make this work?

Spending too much time on any or all of these questions, of course, can lead you into Hamlet's trap, and the opportunity for courage may pass you by. At the same time, too little consideration may result in an o'er-hasty leap. It's important to remember that courageous action in business is for the most part deliberative. Real emergencies are rare. Time may well be on your side.

Before you make your move, it's critical to marshal sufficient support, information, or evidence to improve your odds of success. The sisters Cori and Kerri Rigsby were veteran employees of E.A. Renfroe, a firm that helps State Farm and other insurance companies adjust disaster claims. Following an influx of claims by Hurricane Katrina victims, the Rigsbys found indications that State Farm was pressuring engineers to alter their conclusions about storm damage so that policyholders' claims could be denied. The sisters could have gone public with the first or second piece of evidence, but they were wise enough to know that they needed much more. They spent months collecting 15,000 pages' worth of internal reports, memos, e-mails, and claims, which they turned over to federal and state regulators. They then went to work as consultants for the Scruggs Katrina Group, which was organized to sue insurance companies on behalf of thousands of policyholders.

My research indicates that those who act courageously in business settings have an instinct for opportunity. They read situations quickly, but they are never
reckless. If they sense that the emotional climate is not
right for a frontal assault, or that history or politics raises
insurmountable obstacles, they pause, reflect, and consider another time or route. If they feel outmatched or
lack the skill or stamina to go the distance, they continue
to gather their resources and wait for a more propitious
moment. Choosing the right time is the most difficult
part of the courage calculation; it takes a deep sensitivity
to one's surroundings and a great deal of patience.

Developing Contingency Plans

Faced with having to take a risk, most people make only
one attempt: They ring the doorbell, and if a response is
not forthcoming, they give up and go away. Those who
accomplish their primary and secondary goals try knocking at the back door, tapping at a window, or even
returning a second time.

Winning in risky situations often requires being what
you haven't been, thinking as you haven't thought, and
acting as you haven't acted. The better developed your
contingency plans are, the likelier it is you'll achieve your
primary and secondary goals. But before deciding how to
proceed, it's important to account for possible failure. If
you don't meet your objective, what then? Will your
team lose credibility? Will you think about resigning? If
not, how might you salvage your job or reputation? Can
failure be converted into something positive?

Contingency planning is really about resourcefulness.
People who take bold risks and succeed are versatile
thinkers; they ready themselves with alternative routes.
Tania Modic, for example, decided that if things went

badly after her risky move, she would call the bank chairman, with whom she had a good rapport, and explain her decision. She could promise never to step out of line again. She figured that asking forgiveness after the fact was a better option than asking permission beforehand. She believed that if she got into trouble, one good word from the chairman would help her case. She even invited him to listen in on the phone call in which her superiors asked her to explain herself. As it turned out, she didn't need the chairman's support; but knowing that she could probably get it had emboldened her.

Courageous managers prepare themselves for any eventuality, including worst-case scenarios. Alison May was one of a group of stock traders attending a conflict-resolution workshop. All the attendees were young, bright, and capable, but also mutually antagonistic and unrelentingly competitive. They were courteous during the workshop, even flattering one another; but their level of conflict had reached pathological proportions, and May was disgusted by the vicious backbiting and hypocrisy of the group. She spoke up: "Who are we kidding? We despise each other most of the time." Looking directly into the eyes of her colleagues, she proceeded to describe their most flagrant transgressions. Then one red-faced trader pointed a finger at another and the venom spilled. Attacks and counterattacks flooded the air, but the group was honestly confronting its demons. Progress was made and remedies agreed to, all because May stepped up to the plate.

May had thought long and hard about the worst possible consequence: that her candor would motivate the others to get her fired. She knew that she could get another job. In fact, her most liberating contingency plan was, as she put it, to "work at McDonald's flipping burgers" rather than remain in the vipers' pit. This gave her the freedom to speak up. To her relief, the group didn't hold her outburst against her. On some level, its members were relieved to have the issues aired, and the senior VP at the workshop was impressed. May went on to become the CFO of the outdoor-clothing retailer Patagonia and, later, the CEO of the gift-catalogue company RedEnvelope.

ALISON MAY ONCE undertook an exercise that can be useful to anyone wishing to cultivate professional courage. She wrote down the five most critical conditions for any future endeavor: that she be doing meaningful work she loved; that she be proud of the company for which she worked and proud to tell people she worked there; that at least half the company's employees and senior managers be women; that the company have a higher mission and a product that was fun, valuable, or beneficial to society; and that the company's values match her own. Throughout her career, she has measured courageous risks against this template.

In the end, courage in business rests on priorities that serve a personal, an organizational, or a societal philosophy. When this philosophy is buttressed by clear, obtainable primary and secondary goals, an evaluation of their importance, a favorable power base, a careful assessment of risks versus benefits, appropriate timing, and well-developed contingency plans, managers are better empowered to make bold moves that serve their organizations, their careers, and their own sense of personal worth.

Originally published in January 2007
Reprint R0701E

How to Stay Stuck in the Wrong Career

HERMINIA IBARRA

Executive Summary

EVERYONE KNOWS a story about a talented businessperson who has lost his passion for work, or a person who ditched a 20-year career to pursue something completely different and is the happier for it. "Am I doing what is right for me, or should I change direction?" is one of the most pressing questions for today's midcareer professional.

A true change of direction is hard to swing. Many academics and career counselors contend that the problem lies in basic human behavior: We fear change and don't want to make sacrifices. But author Herminia Ibarra suggests another explanation. People most often fail, she says, because they take the wrong approach to finding new careers. Indeed, the conventional wisdom on how to change careers is a prescription for how to stay put.

Most of us have heard that the key to a successful career change is figuring out what we want to do next, then acting on that knowledge. But change actually happens the other way around. Doing comes first, knowing second, because changing careers means redefining our *working identity*—our sense of self in our professional roles, what we convey about ourselves to others and, ultimately, how we live our working lives. Who we are and what we do are tightly connected, the result of years of action. And to change that connection, we must first resort to action—exactly what the conventional wisdom cautions us against.

Many successful career changers use a test-and-learn model of change, putting their possible identities into practice and then working and crafting them until the identities are sufficiently grounded in experience to guide more decisive steps. To make a break with the past, we must venture into the unknown.

EVERYONE KNOWS A STORY about a smart and talented businessperson who has lost his or her passion for work, who no longer looks forward to going to the office yet remains stuck without a visible way out. Most everyone knows a story, too, about a person who ditched a 20-year career to pursue something completely different—the lawyer who gave it all up to become a writer or the auditor who quit her accounting firm to start her own toy company—and is the happier for it.

"Am I doing what is right for me, or should I change direction?" is one of the most pressing questions in the midcareer professional's mind today. The numbers of people making major career changes, not to mention those just thinking about it, have risen significantly over the last decade and continue to grow. But the difference between the person who yearns for change yet stays put and the person who takes the leap to find renewed fulfillment at midcareer is not what you might expect. Consider the following examples:

Susan Fontaine made a clean break with her unfulfilling past as partner and head of the strategy practice at a top consulting firm. But the former management consultant—her name, like the names of the other people I studied, has been changed for this article—had not yet had the time to figure out a future direction. When a close client offered her the top strategy job at a *Financial Times* 100 firm, she took it. She was ready for change, and the opportunity was too good to pass up. To her dismay, this position—though perfect according to what she calls "the relentless logic of a post-MBA CV"—was no different from her old job in all the aspects she had been seeking to change. Two weeks into the new role, she realized she had made a terrible mistake.

After a four-week executive education program at a top business school, Harris Roberts, a regulatory affairs director at a major health care firm, was ready for change. He wanted bottom-line responsibility, and he itched to put into practice some of the cutting-edge ideas he had learned in the program. His longtime mentor, the company's CEO, had promised, "When you come back, we'll give you a business unit." But upon Harris's return, a complicated new product introduction delayed the long-awaited transition. He was needed in his old role, so he was asked to postpone his dream. As always, Harris put the company first. But he was disappointed; there was no challenge anymore. Resigned to waiting it out, he created for himself a "network of mentors," senior members of the firm whom he enlisted to guide his development and help him try to land the coveted general management role. Eighteen months later, he was still doing essentially the same job.

A milestone birthday, upheaval in his personal life, and a negative performance evaluation—the first of his career—combined to make a "snapping point" for Gary McCarthy. After business school, the former investment banker and consultant had taken a job at a blue-chip firm by default, biding his time until he found his "true passion." Now, he decided, it was time to make a proactive career choice. Determined to get it right, Gary did all the correct things. He started with a career psychologist who gave him a battery of tests to help him figure out his work interests and values. He talked to headhunters, friends, and family and read best-selling books on career change. By his own account, none of the advice was very useful. He researched possible industries and companies. He made two lists: completely different professions involving things he was passionate about and variations on what he was already doing. A year later, a viable alternative had yet to materialize.

When I consider the experiences of these people and dozens of others I have studied over the past few years, there can be no doubt: Despite the rhetoric, a true change of direction is very hard to swing. This isn't because managers or professionals are typically unwilling to change; on the contrary, many make serious attempts to reinvent themselves, devoting large amounts of time and energy to the process at great professional and personal risk. But despite heroic efforts, they remain stuck in the wrong careers, not living up to their potential and sacrificing professional fulfillment.

Many academics and career counselors observe this inertia and conclude that the problem lies in basic human motives: We fear change, lack readiness, are unwilling to make sacrifices, sabotage ourselves. My in-depth research (see the insert "Studying Career Change" at the end of this article for an explanation of my methods) leads me to a different conclusion: People most often fail because they go about it all wrong. Indeed, the conventional wisdom on how to change careers is in fact a prescription for how to stay put. The problem lies in our methods, not our motives.

In my study, I saw many people try a conventional approach and then languish for months, if not years. But by taking a different tack, one I came to call the practice of *working identity,* they eventually found their way to brand-new careers. The phrase "working identity," of course, carries two meanings. It is, first, our sense of self in our professional roles, what we convey about ourselves to others and, ultimately, how we live our working lives. But it can also denote action—a process of applying effort to reshape that identity. Working our identity, I found, is a matter of skill, not personality, and therefore can be learned by almost anyone seeking professional renewal. But first we have to be willing to abandon everything we have ever been taught about making sound career decisions.

A Three-Point Plan

We like to think that the key to a successful career change is knowing what we want to do next, then using that knowledge to guide our actions. But studying people in the throes of the career change process (as opposed to afterward, when hindsight is always 20/20) led me to a startling conclusion: Change actually happens the other way around. Doing comes first, knowing second.

Why? Because changing careers means redefining our working identity. Career change follows a first-act-and-then-think sequence because who we are and what we do are tightly connected, the result of years of action; to change that connection, we must also resort to action—exactly what the conventional wisdom cautions us against.

Conventional career change methods—Susan's "logical" CV progression, Harris's networking, and Gary's planning—are all part of what I call the "plan and implement" model of change. It goes like this: First, determine with as much clarity and certainty as possible what you really want to do. Next, use that knowledge to identify jobs or fields in which your passions can be coupled with your skills and experience. Seek advice from the people who know you best and from professionals in tune with the market. Then simply implement the resulting action steps. Change is seen as a one-shot deal: The plan-and-implement approach cautions us against making a move before we know exactly where we are going.

It all sounds reasonable, and it is a reassuring way to proceed. Yet my research suggests that proceeding this way will lead to the most disastrous of results, which is to say no result. So if your deepest desire is to remain indefinitely in a career that grates on your nerves or stifles your self-expression, simply adhere to that conventional wisdom, presented below as a foolproof, three-point plan.

Know Thyself

Like Gary McCarthy, most of us are taught to begin a
career change with a quest for self-knowledge. Knowing,
in theory, comes from self-reflection, in solitary introspection or with the help of standardized questionnaires
and certified professionals. Learning whether we are
introverted or extroverted, whether we prefer to work in
a structured and methodical environment or in chaos,
whether we place greater value on impact or income
helps us avoid jobs that will again prove unsatisfying.
Having reached an understanding of his or her tempera-
ment, needs, competencies, core values, and priorities, a
person can go out and find a job or organization that
matches.

Gary did all these things. Armed with his test results,
he researched promising companies and industries and
networked with a lot of people to get leads and referrals.
He made two lists of possibilities: "conformist" and "non-
conformist." But what happened from there, and what
consumed 90% of the year he spent looking for a new
career, is what the conventional models leave out—a lot
of trial and error.

Gary started with several rounds of talking with traditional companies and headhunters. Next, he tried to turn
a passion or a hobby into a career: He and his wife wrote
a business plan for a wine-tour business. The financials
were not great, so they dropped it. Next, he pursued his
true fantasy career: Gary got certified as a scuba instruc-
tor and looked into the purchase of a dive operation.
He soon learned, though, that his dream job was unlikely
to hold his interest over the long term (and thus was
not worth the economic sacrifice). So he went back
to the headhunters and traditional companies, only to

reconfirm that he did not want what they had to offer. Next, he identified entrepreneurs he admired and looked for ways to get his foot in their doors. He explored free-lancing, trying to get short-term projects in exciting young companies. But a precise match did not materialize.

Certainly the common practice of looking back over our careers and identifying what we liked and disliked, what we found satisfying and not satisfying, can be a useful tool. But too often this practice is rooted in the profound misconception that it is possible to discover one's "true self," when the reality is that none of us has such an essence. (See the insert "Our Many Possible Selves" at the end of this article for a discussion of why one's true self is so elusive.) Intense introspection also poses the danger that a potential career changer will get stuck in the realm of daydreams. Either the fantasy never finds a match in a real-world, paycheck-producing job or, unlike Gary, we remain emotionally attached to a fantasy career that we do not realize we have outgrown.

We learn who we have become—in practice, not in theory—by testing fantasy and reality, not by "looking inside." Knowing oneself is crucial, but it is usually the outcome of—and not a first input to—the reinvention process. Worse, starting out by trying to identify one's true self often causes paralysis. While we wait for the flash of blinding insight, opportunities pass us by. To launch ourselves anew, we need to get out of our heads. We need to *act.*

Consult Trusted Advisers

If you accept the conventional wisdom that career change begins with self-knowledge and proceeds through an objective scrutiny of the available choices, who should you turn to for guidance? Conventional wisdom has it that you should look to those who know you best and those who know the market. Friends and family—with whom you share a long history—can offer insight into your true nature, and they have your best interests at heart; professionals add a dose of pragmatism, keeping you grounded in the realities of the marketplace.

In times of change and uncertainty, we naturally take comfort in our enduring connections with friends and family. But when it comes to reinventing ourselves, the people who know us best are the ones most likely to hinder rather than help us. They may wish to be supportive, but they tend to reinforce—or even desperately try to preserve—the old identities we are trying to shed. Early in his career, Gary discovered that his close circle would not be much help. "I wanted to do something different but was shocked to realize that people were already pigeonholing me," he says. "I tried to brainstorm with friends and family about what other things I might do. All the ideas that came back were a version of 'Well, you could get a middle management job in a finance department of a company.' Or 'You could become a trainee in a management program.'" John Alexander, an investment banker hoping to make a go of fiction writing, reports that he had often discussed his career predicament with his friends and family. "They would tend to say, 'I can see why writing might be interesting, but you've got a very good job, and do you really want to jeopardize that?'"

Mentors and close coworkers, though well meaning, can also unwittingly hold us back. Take Harris Roberts, the health care company director who wanted to assume a general management role. The people around him, who were invested in his staying put, only mirrored his normal doubts about moving outside his comfort zone. His mentors cared about him and held the power to make his desired change a reality. But they made a fence, not a gateway, blocking the moves that would lead to career change. By talking only to people who inhabited his immediate professional world, people whose ideas for him didn't go beyond the four walls, Harris seriously limited himself. Not only did he lack outside market information, but these coworkers could no more let go of their outdated image of a junior Harris than he himself could.

Headhunters and outplacers, today's career change professionals, can keep us tethered to the past just as effectively. We assume, rightly, that they have the market perspective we lack—but we forget that they are in the business of facilitating incremental moves along an established trajectory. At midcareer, however, many people are no longer looking to "leverage past experience in a different setting." They want to invent their own jobs and escape the shackles of corporate convention, in some cases to do something completely different. What Susan Fontaine, the management consultant, experienced is typical: "I found headhunters unhelpful, basically. I would say, 'Here are my skills; what else might I do?' And they kept saying, 'Why don't you move to Andersen?' or, 'Why don't you try Bain?' All they could suggest was exactly the same thing. I kept saying, 'I'm quite clear I don't want to do that, and if I did want to do that, I would not come to you. I can do that on my own.'"

So if self-assessment, the advice of close ones, and the counsel of change professionals won't do it, then where can we find support for our reinvention? To make a true break with the past, we need to see ourselves in a new light. We need guides who have been there and can understand where we are going. Reaching outside our normal circles to new people, networks, and professional communities is the best way to both break frame and get psychological sustenance.

Think Big

We like to think that we can leap directly from a desire for change to a single decision that will complete our reinvention—the conventional wisdom would say you shouldn't fool yourself with small, superficial adjustments. But trying to tackle the big changes too quickly can be counterproductive. Just as starting the transition by looking for one's true self can cause paralysis rather than progress, trying to make one big move once and for all can prevent real change.

When Susan Fontaine decided to leave her consulting career, it was with good reason. A single mother of two, she was finding the travel and other demands on her personal life increasingly intolerable. She quit her job and resolved to spend some time exploring her options. That resolve vanished, however, when financial pressure coincided with a flattering offer to join the management team of a former client. She accepted the new position only to discover that its demands would be very similar to those of the position she had left. "I thought, 'What have I done?'" she later told me. "I had had the opportunity to leave all that!" By hoping to solve all her problems in one fell swoop, Susan made a change that amounted to no change at all. Two weeks into the new job, she resigned.

As much as we might want to avoid endless procrastination, premature closure is not the answer. It takes time to discover what we truly want to change and to identify the deeply grooved habits and assumptions that are holding us back. The lesson of Susan's story is that trying to make a single bold move can bring us back to square one all too quickly. A longer, less linear transition process may leave us feeling that we are wasting time. But as we will see below, taking smaller steps can allow a richer, more grounded redefinition of our working identity to emerge.

Three Success Stories

Although they floundered, victims of conventional wisdom, Gary McCarthy, Harris Roberts, and Susan Fontaine eventually moved on to a different—and more successful—approach. Gary is now at a media company he admires, working as an internal venture capitalist, a role that allows him to use his skill set in consulting and finance but grants him great creative latitude and total ownership of his results. Harris is president and COO of a growing medical device company and very much involved in setting the strategic direction of his new firm. Susan is working with nonprofits, bringing her strategy expertise to this sector and loving her work.

None of them followed a straight and narrow route. Gary dabbled in wine tours and flirted with buying a scuba diving operation before settling on what his wife called a more normal path. Harris had his prized general management role snatched from under him a second time as the result of a corporate restructuring. He considered leaving for a biotech start-up but realized that he simply did not have the appetite for such a risky move. Susan set up temporarily as a freelance consultant, landing traditional consulting projects to pay the bills and using her discretionary time to explore a more varied portfolio of assignments.

Their experience is typical. Nearly everyone who tries to figure out a next career takes a long time to find the one that is truly right. Most career transitions take about three years. It is rarely a linear path: We take two steps forward and one step back, and where we end up often surprises us.

Working Identity

Once we start questioning not just whether we are in the right job or organization today but also what we thought we wanted for the future, the job search methods we have all been taught fail us. But that doesn't mean we must resign ourselves to a random process governed by factors outside our control—a life crisis that forces us to reprioritize, an unexpected job offer. There is an alternative method that works according to a different logic than the plan-and-implement approach. Gary, Harris, and Susan, as well as many other successful career changers I have observed, shared this method, which I call the "test and learn" model of change. During times of transition—when our possible selves are shifting wildly—the only way to create change is by putting our possible identities into practice, working and crafting them until they are sufficiently grounded in experience to guide more decisive steps. (See the exhibit "Test and Learn.")

The test-and-learn approach recognizes that the only way to counter uncertainty and resist the pull of the familiar is to make alternative futures more vivid, more tangible, and more doable. We acquired our old identities in practice. Likewise, we redefine them, in practice, by crafting experiments, shifting connections, and making sense of the changes we are going through. These

Test and Learn

Your working identity is an amalgam of the kind of work you do, the relationships and organizations that form part of your work life, and the story you tell about why you do what you do and how you arrived at that point. Reshaping that identity, therefore, is a matter of making adjustments to all three of those aspects over time. The adjustments happen tentatively and incrementally, so the process can seem disorderly. In fact, it is a logical process of testing, discovering, and adapting that can be learned by almost anyone seeking professional renewal.

Crafting experiments

Working identity is defined by what we do, the professional activities that engage us.	Try out new activities and professional roles on a small scale before making a major commitment to a different path.

Shifting connections

Working identity is also defined by the company we keep, our working relationships, and the professional groups to which we belong.	Develop contacts that can open doors to new worlds, and look for role models and new reference groups to guide and benchmark your progress.

Making sense

Working identity is also defined by the formative events in our lives and the stories that link who we were and who we will become.	Find or create catalysts and triggers for change, and use them as occasions to rework your life story.

three common practices lie at the heart of the most disparate of career changes, lending logic to what can look like chance occurrences and disorderly behavior.

CRAFTING EXPERIMENTS

By far the biggest mistake people make when trying to change careers is delaying the first step until they have settled on a destination. This error is undermining because the only way we figure out what we really want to do is by giving it a try. Understandably, most people are reluctant to leap into the unknown. We must test our fantasies—otherwise, they remain just that. I discovered that most people create new working identities on the side at first, by getting involved in extracurricular ventures and weekend projects.

Crafting experiments refers to the practice of creating these side projects. Their great advantage is that we can try out new professional roles on a limited scale without compromising our current jobs or having to leap into new positions too quickly. In almost every instance of successful change that I have observed, the person had already been deeply engaged in the new career for quite some time.

There are many ways to set up experiments that work. Newly resolved to explore a range of possibilities, Susan took freelancing assignments in her old line of work and did pro bono work for charities as her lifeline to get her through this difficult period. Through that work, she began to develop contacts that led to paid charity consulting. Gradually, she became immersed in nonprofits, a sector she had never expected to find a career in. And she found herself enjoying freelancing. Today, she is working with the largest UK consulting firm that specializes in charities, and she has this to say: "All I hope is that I never again make the mistake of jumping before giving myself the chance to explore what I really want to do."

Other people use temporary assignments, outside contracts, advisory work, and moonlighting to get experience or build skills in new industries. Thanks to a temporary stint at the helm of his division, Harris got over his fear, which had silently plagued him for years, that he lacked the finance and cross-functional background necessary to be a good general manager. This concrete experience, more than any amount of self-reflection, helped him envision himself as a general manager. Taking courses or picking up training and credentials in a new area is still another way of experimenting. For many of the people in my study, an executive program, sabbatical, or extended vacation improved their capacity to move in a new direction. These breaks are powerful because they force us to step back from the daily routine while engaging us with new people and activities.

SHIFTING CONNECTIONS

Consider how common it is for employees to say of their companies, "There is no one here I want to be like." At midcareer, our desire for change is rarely about only the work we do; it is perhaps more importantly about changing our working relationships so they are more satisfying and inspiring. Shifting connections refers to the practice of finding people who can help us see and grow into our new selves. For most successful career changers I have observed, a guiding figure or new professional community helped to light the way and cushion the eventual leap.

Finding a new job always requires networking outside our usual circles. We get ideas and job leads by branching out. Gary, for example, used his alumni and company networks quite successfully. It was an ex-employee of his company—someone he didn't know personally—who got him the temporary project at his current company. But what clinched his decision, what made this job different from all the other conformist roles he had considered, was the opportunity to work for a role model he had long admired and from whom he could learn the ropes.

Seeking refuge in close working relationships is natural in times of change and uncertainty. But Harris made a classic mistake in turning to an old mentor, Alfred, who was too invested in Harris remaining the unsure protégé to give him room to grow. Harris's way out of this "codependent" relationship came via a person he had met casually at a professional conference. Gerry, the company founder who later hired Harris as his COO, initially approached Harris for regulatory advice. Eventually, they developed an informal consulting relationship. In Gerry, Harris found a person who believed in his potential as a general manager and offered a different kind of close, interdependent working relationship: "It was such a contrast to my relationship with Alfred," Harris says. "It's not as paternal. Gerry knows things I need to learn—things that relate to creative financing, ways to raise money—but he also needs to learn from me. He doesn't know how to run a company, and I do. He's looking to me to teach him what's necessary to develop an organization, to build a foundation. I think I can learn a lot from Gerry, but it's a more mature and more professional relationship than I had with Alfred."

To make a break with the past, we must venture into unknown networks—and not just for job leads. Often it is strangers who are best equipped to help us see who we are becoming.

MAKING SENSE

In the middle of the confusion about which way to go, many of us hope for one event that will clarify everything, that will transform our stumbling moves into a coherent trajectory. Julio Gonzales, a doctor trying to leave the practice of medicine, put it like this: "I was waiting for an epiphany—I wake up in the middle of the night and the Angel of Mercy tells me *this* is what I should do." The third working identity practice, making sense, refers to creating our own triggers for change: infusing events—the momentous and the mundane— with special meaning and weaving them into a story about who we are becoming.

Every person who has changed careers has a story about the moment of truth. For John Alexander, the would-be author I've mentioned, the moment of truth came when, on a whim, he visited an astrologer. To his surprise, the first thing she said to him was, "I'm glad I haven't been *you* for the last two or three years. You have been undergoing a painful internal tug-of-war between two opposing factions. One side wants stability, economic well-being, and social status, and the other craves artistic expression, maybe as a writer or an impresario. You may wish to believe that there can be reconciliation between these two. I tell you, there cannot be." Another career changer, a woman who had grown increasingly frustrated as an executive in a high-tech start-up, said, "One day my husband just asked me, 'Are you happy? If you are, that's great. But you don't *look* happy.' His question prompted me to reconsider what I was doing."

It would be easy to believe from such accounts that career changes have their geneses in such moments. But the moment of insight is an effect, not a cause, of change. Across my many interviews, a striking discovery was that such moments tended to occur late in the transition process, only after much trial and tribulation. Rather than catalyzing change, defining moments helped people make sense of changes that had long been unfolding.

Trigger events don't just jolt us out of our habitual routines, they are the necessary pegs on which to hang our reinvention stories. Arranging life events into a coherent story is one of the subtlest, yet most demanding, challenges of career reinvention. To reinvent oneself is to rework one's story. At the start of a career transition, when all we have is a laundry list of diffuse ideas, it unsettles us that we have no story. It disturbs us to find so many different options appealing, and we worry that the same self who once chose what we no longer want to do might again make a bad choice. Without a story that explains why we must change, the external audience to whom we are selling our reinvention remains dubious, and we, too, feel unsettled and uncertain.

Good stories develop in the telling and retelling, by being put into the public sphere even before they are fully formed. Instead of being embarrassed about having visited an astrologer, for example, John told everyone his story and even wrote about it in a newspaper column. The closer he got to finding his creative outlet, the more the episode made sense and the less often his story elicited the "Why would you want to do that?" reaction. By making public declarations about what we seek and about the common thread that binds our old and new selves, we clarify our intentions and improve our ability to enlist others' support.

The Road Now Taken

Most of us know what we are trying to escape: the lock-step of a narrowly defined career, inauthentic or unstimulating work, numbing corporate politics, a lack of time for life outside of work. Finding an alternative that truly fits, like finding one's mission in life, cannot be accomplished overnight. It takes time, perseverance, and hard work. But effort isn't enough; a sound method and the skill to put it into practice are also required.

The idea of working one's identity flies in the face of everything we have always been told about choosing careers. It asks us to devote the greater part of our time and energy to action rather than reflection, to doing instead of planning. It tells us to give up the search for a ten-point plan and to accept instead a crooked path. But what appears to be a mysterious, road-to-Damascus process is actually a learning-by-doing practice that any of us can adopt. We start by taking action.

Our Many Possible Selves

WHAT IS IDENTITY? Most traditional definitions—the ones that form the foundation for most career advice—are based on the notion of an "inner core" or a "true self." By early adulthood, these theories suggest, a person has formed a relatively stable personality structure, defined by his or her aptitudes, preferences, and values. Excavating this true self—often forgotten in a dead-end pursuit of fame, fortune, or social approval—should be the starting point of any career reorientation, according to conventional wisdom. With the appropriate self-knowledge, obtained via introspection and psychological testing, a person can more easily search for the right "match" and avoid the mistakes of the past. This true-self definition corresponds perfectly to the plan-and-implement method—once we find the self, all that remains is execution.

The work of Stanford cognitive psychologist Hazel Markus and other behavioral scientists, however, offers a different definition of identity, one that is more consistent with what I have discovered: We are many selves. And while these selves are defined partly by our histories, they are defined just as powerfully by our present circumstances and our hopes and fears for the future.

Our possible selves—the images and fantasies we all have about who we hope to become, think we should become, or even fear becoming—are at the heart of the career change process. Although conventional wisdom says pain—a self we fear becoming—is the only driver for change, in reality pain can create paralysis. We change only when we have enticing alternatives that we can feel, touch, and taste. That is why working identity, as a practice, is necessarily a process of experimenting, testing, and learning about our possible selves.

Take Gary McCarthy, the former investment banker and consultant profiled in the main article. The set of possible selves he considered is typical in its number and range. It included a "ditch it all and open a tour-guide business in the south of France with my wife" self; a socially respectable "junior partner" self that his parents would have endorsed; a youthful, outdoorsy, "follow your passion" self who renounced convention and wanted to open a scuba business; a "responsible spouse and future parent" self who wanted to make good dual-career decisions; a "corporate drone at age 50, full of regrets" self; an "apprentice" self who learned at the elbow of an admired entrepreneur; and a practical, reasonable, "go to a traditional company where I can combine my backgrounds in banking and consulting" self.

Conventional wisdom would say that the scope of his list of possibilities was evidence that he lacked focus and wasn't ready for change. But within the working identity framework, it was precisely this variety that allowed him to find a truly good fit. Certain possible selves are concrete and tangible, defined by the things we do and the company we keep today; others remain vague and fuzzy, existing only in the realm of private dreams, hypothetical possibilities, and abstract ideas. By bringing the possibilities—both desired and feared, present and future—more sharply into focus, we give ourselves a concrete base of experience from which to choose among them.

Studying Career Change

CERTAIN CAREER TRANSITIONS have been thoroughly studied and are well understood: a move into a position of greater managerial responsibility and organizational status, a transfer to a similar job in a new company or industry, a lateral move into a different work function within a familiar field. But few researchers have investigated how managers and professionals go about making a true change of direction.

My research is an in-depth study of 39 people who changed, or were in the process of trying to change, careers. Determining the magnitude of any work transition is highly subjective. Who, apart from the person who has lived through it, can say whether a shift is radical or incremental? After interviewing dozens of people who were making very different kinds of career moves, I settled on a three-part definition of career change.

Some of the people in my study made significant changes in the context in which they worked, most typically jumping from large, established companies to small, entrepreneurial organizations or to self-employment or between the for-profit and non-profit sectors. Others made major changes in the content of the work, sometimes leaving occupations, such as medicine, law or academia, that they had trained for extensively. The majority made significant changes in both what they did and where they did it, but most important, all experienced a feeling of having reached a crossroad, one that would require psychological change.

My sample ranged in age from 32 to 51, with an average of 41. I chose this range not to coincide with the infamous midlife crisis but to study a group of people with enough experience in one career to make a shift to another high-stakes endeavor. Sixty-five percent of the participants were men. Almost half of the subjects lived and worked outside the United States, mostly in France and the UK. It was a highly credentialed sample: All had college degrees, and about three-fourths held graduate or professional degrees (business, science, law, and so on). They represented all walks of managerial and professional life, including business management, law, finance, academia, medicine, science, and technology.

Some of the interviews were retrospective, with people who had already completed their changes. With people at earlier stages of the transition, I conducted an average of three interviews over two to three years. The interviews were open-ended, typically beginning with: "Tell me about your career to date." Between the interviews, I had e-mail exchanges and telephone conversations with participants to keep track of their progress. I supplemented this core study with many shorter interviews involving a range of career change professionals, including headhunters, venture capitalists, career counselors, and outplacement specialists.

Originally published in December 2002
Reprint 2330

A Survival Guide for Leaders

RONALD A. HEIFETZ AND MARTY LINSKY

Executive Summary

LET'S FACE IT, to lead is to live dangerously. While leadership is often viewed as an exciting and glamorous endeavor, one in which you inspire others to follow you through good times and bad, such a portrayal ignores leadership's dark side: the inevitable attempts to take you out of the game.

This is particularly true when a leader must steer an organization through difficult change. When the status quo is upset, people feel a sense of profound loss and dashed expectations. They may need to undergo a period of feeling incompetent or disloyal. It's no wonder they resist the change and often try to eliminate its visible agent.

This "survival guide" offers a number of techniques—relatively straightforward in concept but difficult to execute—for protecting yourself as you lead such a change initiative. Adapted from the book *Leadership on the Line: Staying Alive Through the Dangers of Leading* (Harvard Business School Press, 2002), the article has two main parts. The first looks outward, offering tactical advice about relating to your organization and the people in it. It is designed to protect you from those who would push you aside before you complete your initiatives. The second looks inward, focusing on your own needs and vulnerabilities. It is designed to keep you from bringing yourself down.

The hard truth is that it is not possible to experience the rewards and joys of leadership without experiencing the pain as well. But staying in the game and bearing that pain is worth it, not only for the positive changes you can make in the lives of others but also for the meaning it gives your own.

T HINK OF THE MANY top executives in recent years who, sometimes after long periods of considerable success, have crashed and burned. Or think of individuals you have known in less prominent positions, perhaps people spearheading significant change initiatives in their organizations, who have suddenly found themselves out of a job. Think about yourself: In exercising leadership, have *you* ever been removed or pushed aside?

Let's face it, to lead is to live dangerously. While leadership is often depicted as an exciting and glamorous endeavor, one in which you inspire others to follow you through good times and bad, such a portrayal ignores leadership's dark side: the inevitable attempts to take you out of the game.

Those attempts are sometimes justified. People in top positions must often pay the price for a flawed strategy or a series of bad decisions. But frequently, something more is at work. We're not talking here about conventional office politics; we're talking about the high-stake risks you face whenever you try to lead an organization through difficult but necessary change. The risks during such times are especially high because change that truly transforms an organization, be it a multibillion-dollar company or a ten-person sales team, demands that people give up things they hold dear: daily habits, loyalties, ways of thinking. In return for these sacrifices, they may be offered nothing more than the possibility of a better future.

We refer to this kind of wrenching organizational transformation as "adaptive change," something very different from the "technical change" that occupies people in positions of authority on a regular basis. Technical problems, while often challenging, can be solved applying existing know-how and the organization's current problem-solving processes. Adaptive problems resist these kinds of solutions because they require individuals throughout the organization to alter their ways; as the people themselves are the problem, the solution lies with them. (See the insert "Adaptive Versus Technical Change: Whose Problem Is It?" at the end of this article.) Responding to an adaptive challenge with a technical fix may have some short-term appeal. But to make real progress, sooner or later those who lead must ask themselves and the people in the organization to face a set of deeper issues—and to accept a solution that may require turning part or all of the organization upside down.

It is at this point that danger lurks. And most people who lead in such a situation—swept up in the action, championing a cause they believe in—are caught unawares. Over and over again, we have seen courageous souls blissfully ignorant of an approaching threat until it was too late to respond.

The hazard can take numerous forms. You may be attacked directly in an attempt to shift the debate to your character and style and avoid discussion of your initiative. You may be marginalized, forced into the position of becoming so identified with one issue that your broad authority is undermined. You may be seduced by your supporters and, fearful of losing their approval and affection, fail to demand they make the sacrifices needed for the initiative to succeed. You may be diverted from your goal by people overwhelming you with the day-to-day details of carrying it out, keeping you busy and preoccupied.

Each one of these thwarting tactics—whether done consciously or not—grows out of people's aversion to the organizational disequilibrium created by your initiative. By attempting to undercut you, people strive to restore order, maintain what is familiar to them, and protect themselves from the pains of adaptive change. They want to be comfortable again, and you're in the way.

So how do you protect yourself? Over a combined 50 years of teaching and consulting, we have asked ourselves that question time and again—usually while watching top-notch and well-intentioned folks get taken out of the game. On occasion, the question has become painfully personal; we as individuals have been knocked off course or out of the action more than once in our own leadership efforts. So we are offering what we hope are some pragmatic answers that grow out of these observations and experiences. We should note that while our advice clearly applies to senior executives, it also applies to people trying to lead change initiatives from positions of little or no formal organizational authority.

This "survival guide" has two main parts. The first looks outward, offering tactical advice about relating to your organization and the people in it. It is designed to protect you from those trying to push you aside before you complete your initiative. The second looks inward, focusing on your own human needs and vulnerabilities. It is designed to keep you from bringing yourself down.

A Hostile Environment

Leading major organizational change often involves radically reconfiguring a complex network of people, tasks, and institutions that have achieved a kind of modus vivendi, no matter how dysfunctional it appears to you. When the status quo is upset, people feel a sense of profound loss and dashed expectations. They may go through a period of feeling incompetent or disloyal. It's no wonder they resist the change or try to eliminate its visible agent. We offer here a number of techniques— relatively straightforward in concept but difficult to execute—for minimizing these external threats.

OPERATE IN AND ABOVE THE FRAY

The ability to maintain perspective in the midst of action is critical to lowering resistance. Any military officer knows the importance of maintaining the capacity for reflection, especially in the "fog of war." Great athletes must simultaneously play the game and observe it as a whole. We call this skill "getting off the dance floor and going to the balcony," an image that captures the mental activity of stepping back from the action and asking, "What's really going on here?"

Leadership is an improvisational art. You may be guided by an overarching vision, clear values, and a strategic plan, but what you actually do from moment to moment cannot be scripted. You must respond as events unfold. To use our metaphor, you have to move back and forth from the balcony to the dance floor, over and over again throughout the days, weeks, months, and years. While today's plan may make sense now, tomorrow you'll discover the unanticipated effects of today's actions and have to adjust accordingly. Sustaining good leadership, then, requires first and foremost the capacity to see what is happening to you and your initiative as it is happening and to understand how today's turns in the road will affect tomorrow's plans.

But taking a balcony perspective is extremely tough to do when you're fiercely engaged down below, being pushed and pulled by the events and people around you—and doing some pushing and pulling of your own. Even if you are able to break away, the practice of stepping back and seeing the big picture is complicated by several factors. For example, when you get some distance, you still must accurately interpret what you see and hear. This is easier said than done. In an attempt to avoid difficult change, people will naturally, even unconsciously, defend their habits and ways of thinking. As you seek input from a broad range of people, you'll constantly need to be aware of these hidden agendas. You'll also need to observe your own actions; seeing yourself objectively as you look down from the balcony is perhaps the hardest task of all.

Fortunately, you can learn to be both an observer and a participant at the same time. When you are sitting in a meeting, practice by watching what is happening while it is happening—even as you are part of what is happening. Observe the relationships and see how people's attention to one another can vary: supporting, thwarting, or listening. Watch people's body language. When you make a point, resist the instinct to stay perched on the edge of your seat, ready to defend what you said. A technique as simple as pushing your chair a few inches away from the table after you speak may provide the literal as well as metaphorical distance you need to become an observer.

COURT THE UNCOMMITTED

It's tempting to go it alone when leading a change initiative. There's no one to dilute your ideas or share the glory, and it's often just plain exciting. It's also foolish. You need to recruit partners, people who can help protect you from attacks and who can point out potentially fatal flaws in your strategy or initiative. Moreover, you are far less vulnerable when you are out on the point with a bunch of folks rather than alone. You also need to keep the opposition close. Knowing what your opponents are thinking can help you challenge them more effectively and thwart their attempts to upset your agenda—or allow you to borrow ideas that will improve your initiative. Have coffee once a week with the person most dedicated to seeing you fail.

But while relationships with allies and opponents are essential, the people who will determine your success are often those in the middle, the uncommitted who nonetheless are wary of your plans. They have no substantive stake in your initiative, but they do have a stake in the comfort, stability, and security of the status quo. They've seen change agents come and go, and they know that your initiative will disrupt their lives and make their futures uncertain. You want to be sure that this general uneasiness doesn't evolve into a move to push you aside.

These people will need to see that your intentions are serious—for example, that you are willing to let go of those who can't make the changes your initiative requires. But people must also see that you understand the loss you are asking them to accept. You need to name the loss, be it a change in time-honored work routines or an overhaul of the company's core values, and explicitly acknowledge the resulting pain. You might do this through a series of simple statements, but it often requires something more tangible and public—recall Franklin Roosevelt's radio "fireside chats" during the Great Depression—to convince people that you truly understand.

Beyond a willingness to accept casualties and acknowledge people's losses, two very personal types of action can defuse potential resistance to you and your initiatives. The first is practicing what you preach. In 1972, Gene Patterson took over as editor of the *St. Petersburg Times.* His mandate was to take the respected regional newspaper to a higher level, enhancing its reputation for fine writing while becoming a fearless and hard-hitting news source. This would require major changes not only in the way the community viewed the newspaper but also in the way *Times* reporters thought about themselves and their roles. Because prominent organizations and individuals would no longer be spared warranted criticism, reporters would sometimes be angrily rebuked by the subjects of articles.

Several years after Patterson arrived, he attended a party at the home of the paper's foreign editor. Driving home, he pulled up to a red light and scraped the car

next to him. The police officer called to the scene
charged Patterson with driving under the influence.
Patterson phoned Bob Haiman, a veteran *Times* newsman who had just been appointed executive editor, and
insisted that a story on his arrest be run. As Haiman
recalls, he tried to talk Patterson out of it, arguing that
DUI arrests that didn't involve injuries were rarely
reported, even when prominent figures were involved.
Patterson was adamant, however, and insisted that the
story appear on page one.

Patterson, still viewed as somewhat of an outsider at
the paper, knew that if he wanted his employees to follow the highest journalistic standards, he would have to
display those standards, even when it hurt. Few leaders
are called upon to disgrace themselves on the front page
of a newspaper. But adopting the behavior you expect
from others—whether it be taking a pay cut in tough
times or spending a day working next to employees on a
reconfigured production line—can be crucial in getting
buy-in from people who might try to undermine your
initiative.

The second thing you can do to neutralize potential
opposition is to acknowledge your own responsibility
for whatever problems the organization currently faces.
If you have been with the company for some time,
whether in a position of senior authority or not, you've
likely contributed in some way to the current mess.
Even if you are new, you need to identify areas of your
own behavior that could stifle the change you hope
to make.

In our teaching, training, and consulting, we often ask
people to write or talk about a leadership challenge they
currently face. Over the years, we have read and heard
literally thousands of such challenges. Typically, in the

first version of the story, the author is nowhere to be found. The underlying message: "If only other people would shape up, I could make progress here." But by too readily pointing your finger at others, you risk making yourself a target. Remember, you are asking people to move to a place where they are frightened to go. If at the same time you're blaming them for having to go there, they will undoubtedly turn against you.

In the early 1990s, Leslie Wexner, founder and CEO of the Limited, realized the need for major changes at the company, including a significant reduction in the workforce. But his consultant told him that something else had to change: long-standing habits that were at the heart of his self-image. In particular, he had to stop treating the company as if it were his family. The indulgent father had to become the chief personnel officer, putting the right people in the right jobs and holding them accountable for their work. "I was an athlete trained to be a baseball player," Wexner recalled during a recent speech at Harvard's Kennedy School. "And one day, someone tapped me on the shoulder and said, 'Football.' And I said, 'No, I'm a baseball player.' And he said, 'Football.' And I said, 'I don't know how to play football. I'm not 6'4", and I don't weigh 300 pounds.' But if no one values baseball anymore, the baseball player will be out of business. So I looked into the mirror and said, 'Schlemiel, nobody wants to watch baseball. Make the transformation to football.'" His personal makeover—shedding the role of forgiving father to those widely viewed as not holding their own—helped sway other employees to back a corporate makeover. And his willingness to change helped protect him from attack during the company's long—and generally successful—turnaround period.

COOK THE CONFLICT

Managing conflict is one of the greatest challenges a leader of organizational change faces. The conflict may involve resistance to change, or it may involve clashing viewpoints about how the change should be carried out. Often, it will be latent rather than palpable. That's because most organizations are allergic to conflict, seeing it primarily as a source of danger, which it certainly can be. But conflict is a necessary part of the change process and, if handled properly, can serve as the engine of progress.

Thus, a key imperative for a leader trying to achieve significant change is to manage people's passionate differences in a way that diminishes their destructive potential and constructively harnesses their energy. Two techniques can help you achieve this. First, create a secure place where the conflicts can freely bubble up. Second, control the temperature to ensure that the conflict doesn't boil over—and burn you in the process.

The vessel in which a conflict is simmered—in which clashing points of view mix, lose some of their sharpness, and ideally blend into consensus—will look and feel quite different in different contexts. It may be a protected physical space, perhaps an off-site location where an outside facilitator helps a group work through its differences. It may be a clear set of rules and processes that give minority voices confidence that they will be heard without having to disrupt the proceedings to gain attention. It may be the shared language and history of an organization that binds people together through trying times. Whatever its form, it is a place or a means to contain the roiling forces unleashed by the threat of major change.

But a vessel can withstand only so much strain before it blows. A huge challenge you face as a leader is keeping your employees' stress at a productive level. The success of the change effort—as well as your own authority and even survival—requires you to monitor your organization's tolerance for heat and then regulate the temperature accordingly.

You first need to raise the heat enough that people sit up, pay attention, and deal with the real threats and challenges facing them. After all, without some distress, there's no incentive to change. You can constructively raise the temperature by focusing people's attention on the hard issues, by forcing them to take responsibility for tackling and solving those issues, and by bringing conflicts occurring behind closed doors out into the open.

But you have to lower the temperature when necessary to reduce what can be counterproductive turmoil. You can turn down the heat by slowing the pace of change or by tackling some relatively straightforward technical aspect of the problem, thereby reducing people's anxiety levels and allowing them to get warmed up for bigger challenges. You can provide structure to the problem-solving process, creating work groups with specific assignments, setting time parameters, establishing rules for decision making, and outlining reporting relationships. You can use humor or find an excuse for a break or a party to temporarily ease tensions. You can speak to people's fears and, more critically, to their hopes for a more promising future. By showing people how the future might look, you come to embody hope rather than fear, and you reduce the likelihood of becoming a lightning rod for the conflict.

The aim of both these tactics is to keep the heat high enough to motivate people but low enough to prevent a disastrous explosion—what we call a "productive range of distress." Remember, though, that most employees will reflexively want you to turn down the heat; their complaints may in fact indicate that the environment is just right for hard work to get done.

We've already mentioned a classic example of managing the distress of fundamental change: Franklin Roosevelt during the first few years of his presidency. When he took office in 1933, the chaos, tension, and anxiety brought on by the Depression ran extremely high. Demagogues stoked class, ethnic, and racial conflict that threatened to tear the nation apart. Individuals feared an uncertain future. So Roosevelt first did what he could to reduce the sense of disorder to a tolerable level. He took decisive and authoritative action—he pushed an extraordinary number of bills through Congress during his fabled first 100 days—and thereby gave Americans a sense of direction and safety, reassuring them that they were in capable hands. In his fireside chats, he spoke to people's anxiety and anger and laid out a positive vision for the future that made the stress of the current crisis bearable and seem a worthwhile price to pay for progress.

But he knew the problems facing the nation couldn't be solved from the White House. He needed to mobilize citizens and get them to dream up, try out, fight over, and ultimately own the sometimes painful solutions that would transform the country and move it forward. To do that, he needed to maintain a certain level of fermentation and distress. So, for example, he orchestrated conflicts over public priorities and programs among the large cast of creative people he brought into the government. By giving the same assignment to two different administrators and refusing to clearly define their roles, he got them to generate new and competing ideas. Roosevelt displayed both the acuity to recognize when the tension in the nation had risen too high and the emotional strength to take the heat and permit considerable anxiety to persist.

PLACE THE WORK WHERE IT BELONGS

Because major change requires people across an entire organization to adapt, you as a leader need to resist the reflex reaction of providing people with the answers. Instead, force yourself to transfer, as Roosevelt did, much of the work and problem solving to others. If you don't, real and sustainable change won't occur. In addition, it's risky on a personal level to continue to hold on to the work that should be done by others.

As a successful executive, you have gained credibility and authority by demonstrating your capacity to solve other people's problems. This ability can be a virtue, until you find yourself faced with a situation in which you cannot deliver solutions. When this happens, all of your habits, pride, and sense of competence get thrown out of kilter because you must mobilize the work of others rather than find the way yourself. By trying to solve an adaptive challenge for people, at best you will reconfigure it as a technical problem and create some short-term relief. But the issue will not have gone away.

In the 1994 National Basketball Association Eastern Conference semifinals, the Chicago Bulls lost to the New York Knicks in the first two games of the best-of-seven series. Chicago was out to prove that it was more than just a one-man team, that it could win without Michael Jordan, who had retired at the end of the previous season.

In the third game, the score was tied at 102 with less than two seconds left. Chicago had the ball and a time-out to plan a final shot. Coach Phil Jackson called for Scottie Pippen, the Bulls' star since Jordan had retired, to make the inbound pass to Toni Kukoc for the final shot. As play was about to resume, Jackson noticed Pippen sitting at the far end of the bench. Jackson asked him whether he was in or out. "I'm out," said Pippen, miffed that he was not tapped to take the final shot. With only four players on the floor, Jackson quickly called another time-out and substituted an excellent passer, the reserve Pete Myers, for Pippen. Myers tossed a perfect pass to Kukoc, who spun around and sank a miraculous shot to win the game.

The Bulls made their way back to the locker room, their euphoria deflated by Pippen's extraordinary act of insubordination. Jackson recalls that as he entered a silent room, he was uncertain about what to do. Should he punish Pippen? Make him apologize? Pretend the whole thing never happened? All eyes were on him. The coach looked around, meeting the gaze of each player, and said, "What happened has hurt us. Now you have to work this out."

Jackson knew that if he took action to resolve the immediate crisis, he would have made Pippen's behavior a matter between coach and player. But he understood that a deeper issue was at the heart of the incident: Who were the Chicago Bulls without Michael Jordan? It wasn't about who was going to succeed Jordan, because no one was; it was about whether the players could jell as a team where no one person dominated and every player was willing to do whatever it took to help. The issue rested with the players, not him, and only they could resolve it. It did not matter what they decided at that moment;

what mattered was that they, not Jackson, did the deciding. What followed was a discussion led by an emotional Bill Cartwright, a team veteran. According to Jackson, the conversation brought the team closer together. The Bulls took the series to a seventh game before succumbing to the Knicks.

Jackson gave the work of addressing both the Pippen and the Jordan issues back to the team for another reason: If he had taken ownership of the problem, he would have become the issue, at least for the moment. In his case, his position as coach probably wouldn't have been threatened. But in other situations, taking responsibility for resolving a conflict within the organization poses risks. You are likely to find yourself resented by the faction that you decide against and held responsible by nearly everyone for the turmoil your decision generates. In the eyes of many, the only way to neutralize the threat is to get rid of you.

Despite that risk, most executives can't resist the temptation to solve fundamental organizational problems by themselves. People expect you to get right in there and fix things, to take a stand and resolve the problem. After all, that is what top managers are paid to do. When you fulfill those expectations, people will call you admirable and courageous—even a "leader"—and that is flattering. But challenging your employees' expectations requires greater courage and leadership.

The Dangers Within

We have described a handful of leadership tactics you can use to interact with the people around you, particularly those who might undermine your initiatives. Those tactics can help advance your initiatives and, just as important, ensure that you remain in a position where you can bring them to fruition. But from our own observations and painful personal experiences, we know that one of the surest ways for an organization to bring you down is simply to let you precipitate your own demise.

In the heat of leadership, with the adrenaline pumping, it is easy to convince yourself that you are not subject to the normal human frailties that can defeat ordinary mortals. You begin to act as if you are indestructible. But the intellectual, physical, and emotional challenges of leadership are fierce. So, in addition to getting on the balcony, you need to regularly step into the inner chamber of your being and assess the tolls those challenges are taking. If you don't, your seemingly indestructible self can self-destruct. This, by the way, is an ideal outcome for your foes—and even friends who oppose your initiative—because no one has to feel responsible for your downfall.

MANAGE YOUR HUNGERS

We all have hungers, expressions of our normal human needs. But sometimes those hungers disrupt our capacity to act wisely or purposefully. Whether inherited or products of our upbringing, some of these hungers may be so strong that they render us constantly vulnerable. More typically, a stressful situation or setting can exaggerate a normal level of need, amplifying our desires and overwhelming our usual self-discipline. Two of the most common and dangerous hungers are the desire for control and the desire for importance.

Everyone wants to have some measure of control over his or her life. Yet some people's need for control is disproportionately high. They might have grown up in a household that was either tightly structured or unusually chaotic; in either case, the situation drove them to become masters at taming chaos not only in their own lives but also in their organizations.

That need for control can be a source of vulnerability. Initially, of course, the ability to turn disorder into order may be seen as an attribute. In an organization facing turmoil, you may seem like a godsend if you are able (and desperately want) to step in and take charge. By lowering the distress to a tolerable level, you keep the kettle from boiling over.

But in your desire for order, you can mistake the means for the end. Rather than ensuring that the distress level in an organization remains high enough to mobilize progress on the issues, you focus on maintaining order as an end in itself. Forcing people to make the difficult trade-offs required by fundamental change threatens a return to the disorder you loathe. Your ability to bring the situation under control also suits the people in the organization, who naturally prefer calm to chaos. Unfortunately, this desire for control makes you vulnerable to, and an agent of, the organization's wish to avoid working through contentious issues. While this may ensure your survival in the short term, ultimately you may find yourself accused, justifiably, of failing to deal with the tough challenges when there was still time to do so.

Most people also have some need to feel important and affirmed by others. The danger here is that you will let this affirmation give you an inflated view of yourself and your cause. A grandiose sense of self-importance often leads to self-deception. In particular, you tend to forget the creative role that doubt—which reveals parts of reality that you wouldn't otherwise see—plays in getting your organization to improve. The absence of doubt leads you to see only that which confirms your own competence, which will virtually guarantee disastrous missteps.

Another harmful side effect of an inflated sense of self-importance is that you will encourage people in the organization to become dependent on you. The higher the level of distress, the greater their hopes and expectations that you will provide deliverance. This relieves them of any responsibility for moving the organization forward. But their dependence can be detrimental not only to the group but to you personally. Dependence can quickly turn to contempt as your constituents discover your human shortcomings.

Two well-known stories from the computer industry illustrate the perils of dependency—and how to avoid them. Ken Olsen, the founder of Digital Equipment Corporation, built the company into a 120,000-person operation that, at its peak, was the chief rival of IBM. A generous man, he treated his employees extraordinarily well and experimented with personnel policies designed to increase the creativity, teamwork, and satisfaction of his workforce. This, in tandem with the company's success over the years, led the company's top management to turn to him as the sole decision maker on all key issues. His decision to shun the personal computer market because of his belief that few people would ever want to own a PC, which seemed reasonable at the time, is generally viewed as the beginning of the end for the company. But that isn't the point; everyone in business makes bad decisions. The point is, Olsen had fostered such an atmosphere of dependence that his decisions were rarely challenged by colleagues—at least not until it was too late.

Contrast that decision with Bill Gates's decision some years later to keep Microsoft out of the Internet business. It didn't take long for him to reverse his stand and launch a corporate overhaul that had Microsoft's delivery of Internet services as its centerpiece. After watching the rapidly changing computer industry and listening carefully to colleagues, Gates changed his mind with no permanent damage to his sense of pride and an enhanced reputation due to his nimble change of course.

ANCHOR YOURSELF

To survive the turbulent seas of a change initiative, you need to find ways to steady and stabilize yourself. First, you must establish a safe harbor where each day you can reflect on the previous day's journey, repair the psychological damage you have incurred, renew your stores of emotional resources, and recalibrate your moral compass. Your haven might be a physical place, such as the kitchen table of a friend's house, or a regular routine, such as a daily walk through the neighborhood. Whatever the sanctuary, you need to use and protect it. Unfortunately, seeking such respite is often seen as a luxury, making it one of the first things to go when life gets stressful and you become pressed for time.

Second, you need a confidant, someone you can talk to about what's in your heart and on your mind without fear of being judged or betrayed. Once the undigested mess is on the table, you can begin to separate, with your confidant's honest input, what is worthwhile from what is simply venting. The confidant, typically not a coworker, can also pump you up when you're down and pull you back to earth when you start taking praise too seriously. But don't confuse confidants with allies: Instead of supporting your current initiative, a confidant simply supports you. A common mistake is to seek a confidant among trusted allies, whose personal loyalty may evaporate when a new issue more important to them than you begins to emerge and take center stage.

Perhaps most important, you need to distinguish between your personal self, which can serve as an anchor in stormy weather, and your professional role, which never will. It is easy to mix up the two. And other people only increase the confusion: Colleagues, subordinates, and even bosses often act as if the role you play is the real you. But that is not the case, no matter how much of yourself—your passions, your values, your talents—you genuinely and laudably pour into your professional role. Ask anyone who has experienced the rude awakening that comes when they leave a position of authority and suddenly find that their phone calls aren't returned as quickly as they used to be.

That harsh lesson holds another important truth that is easily forgotten: When people attack someone in a position of authority, more often than not they are attacking the role, not the person. Even when attacks on you are highly personal, you need to read them primarily as reactions to how you, in your role, are affecting people's lives. Understanding the criticism for what it is prevents it from undermining your stability and sense of self-worth. And that's important because when you feel the sting of an attack, you are likely to become defensive and lash out at your critics, which can precipitate your downfall.

We hasten to add that criticism may contain legitimate points about how you are performing your role. For example, you may have been tactless in raising an issue with your organization, or you may have turned the heat up too quickly on a change initiative. But, at its heart, the criticism is usually about the issue, not you. Through the guise of attacking you personally, people often are simply trying to neutralize the threat they perceive in your point of view. Does anyone ever attack you when you hand out big checks or deliver good news? People attack your personality, style, or judgment when they don't like the message.

When you take "personal" attacks personally, you unwittingly conspire in one of the common ways you can be taken out of action—you make yourself the issue. Contrast the manner in which presidential candidates Gary Hart and Bill Clinton handled charges of philandering. Hart angrily counterattacked, criticizing the scruples of the reporters who had shadowed him. This defensive personal response kept the focus on his behavior. Clinton, on national television, essentially admitted he had strayed, acknowledging his piece of the mess. His strategic handling of the situation allowed him to return the campaign's focus to policy issues. Though both attacks were extremely personal, only Clinton understood that they were basically attacks on positions he represented and the role he was seeking to play.

Do not underestimate the difficulty of distinguishing self from role and responding coolly to what feels like a personal attack—particularly when the criticism comes, as it will, from people you care about. But disciplining yourself to do so can provide you with an anchor that will keep you from running aground and give you the stability to remain calm, focused, and persistent in engaging people with the tough issues.

Why Lead?

We will have failed if this "survival manual" for avoiding the perils of leadership causes you to become cynical or callous in your leadership effort or to shun the challenges of leadership altogether. We haven't touched on the thrill of inspiring people to come up with creative solutions that can transform an organization for the better. We hope we have shown that the essence of leadership lies in the capacity to deliver disturbing news and raise difficult questions in a way that moves people to take up the message rather than kill the messenger. But we haven't talked about the reasons that someone might want to take these risks.

Of course, many people who strive for high-authority positions are attracted to power. But in the end, that isn't enough to make the high stakes of the game worthwhile. We would argue that, when they look deep within themselves, people grapple with the challenges of leadership in order to make a positive difference in the lives of others.

When corporate presidents and vice presidents reach their late fifties, they often look back on careers devoted to winning in the marketplace. They may have succeeded remarkably, yet some people have difficulty making sense of their lives in light of what they have given up. For too many, their accomplishments seem empty. They question whether they should have been more aggressive in questioning corporate purposes or creating more ambitious visions for their companies.

Our underlying assumption in this article is that you can lead *and* stay alive—not just register a pulse, but really be alive. But the classic protective devices of a person in authority tend to insulate them from those qualities that foster an acute experience of living. Cynicism, often dressed up as realism, undermines creativity and daring. Arrogance, often posing as authoritative knowledge, snuffs out curiosity and the eagerness to question. Callousness, sometimes portrayed as the thick skin of experience, shuts out compassion for others.

The hard truth is that it is not possible to know the rewards and joys of leadership without experiencing the pain as well. But staying in the game and bearing that pain is worth it, not only for the positive changes you can make in the lives of others but also for the meaning it gives your own.

Adaptive Versus Technical Change: Whose Problem Is It?

THE IMPORTANCE—and difficulty—of distinguishing between adaptive and technical change can be illustrated with an analogy. When your car has problems, you go to a mechanic. Most of the time, the mechanic can fix the car. But if your car troubles stem from the way a family member drives, the problems are likely to recur. Treating the problems as purely technical ones—taking the car to the mechanic time and again to get it back on the road—masks the real issues. Maybe you need to get your mother to stop drinking and driving, get your grandfather to give up his driver's license, or get your teenager to be more cautious. Whatever the underlying problems, the mechanic can't solve them. Instead, changes in the family need to occur, and that won't be easy. People will resist the moves, even denying that such problems exist. That's because even those not directly affected by an adaptive change typically experience discomfort when someone upsets a group's or an organization's equilibrium.

Such resistance to adaptive change certainly happens in business. Indeed, it's the classic error: Companies treat adaptive challenges as if they were technical problems. For example, executives attempt to improve the bottom line by cutting costs across the board. Not only does this avoid the need to make tough choices about which areas should be trimmed, it also masks the fact that the company's real challenge lies in redesigning its strategy.

Treating adaptive challenges as technical ones permits executives to do what they have excelled at throughout their careers: solve other people's problems. And it allows others in the organization to enjoy the primordial peace of mind that comes from knowing that their commanding officer has a plan to maintain order and stability. After all, the executive doesn't have to instigate—and the people don't have to undergo—uncomfortable change. Most people would agree that, despite the selective pain of a cost-cutting exercise, it is less traumatic than reinventing a company.

Originally published in June 2002
Reprint R0206C

The Right Way to Be Fired

LAURENCE J. STYBEL AND

MARYANNE PEABODY

Executive Summary

NEARLY ALL OF US will lose our jobs sometime, but is there a right way to be terminated? What differentiates fired employees who make the best of their situations from those who do not? One answer is mind-set. Many workers unconsciously hold a "tenure mindset," believing in the promise of employment security. By contrast, other workers hold an "assignment mentality," seeing each job as one in a series of impermanent, career-building stepping-stones. Most corporate board members and CEOs have this latter mind-set and consider their executives to be filling terminal assignments; people who possess this mentality usually rebound swiftly when fired.

But when employees who hold a tenure mind-set are suddenly fired or laid off, the authors say, they can fall into three common traps. Executives who have overidentified with their jobs and feel indispensable to their organizations get caught in the "lost identity" trap; they react to termination with anger and bitterness. In the "lost family" trap, employees possess tight-knit, emotional bonds with coworkers. When terminated, they feel betrayed and rejected. And finally, some introverted executives fall into the "lost ego" trap; they quietly retreat without negotiating fair termination packages and may settle for less satisfying work the next time around.

To prepare for the eventuality of termination, the authors suggest that executives adopt the assignment mind-set at all times. They should keep their social networks alive, include a termination clause in employment contracts, and consider hiring an agent. If warning signs warrant, they might even volunteer to be terminated. By assuming control over the way they are fired, people can gain control over their careers.

EVEN IN THE BEST OF TIMES, executives get fired, and in the worst, they get fired with disquieting frequency. Indeed, as the economy softens, you only have to glance at the newspaper to see layoffs left, right, and center, mainly to cut costs. You can be a top performer today and still lose your job. The question is: Can you lose it the right way?

For 22 years, we have worked closely with more than 500 senior executives in dozens of industries to manage their careers in good times and in bad. Over and over, we have observed how executives react to being fired or laid off. The majority handle termination with dignity, even elegance. They negotiate handsome severance packages, part with their employers on amicable terms, and position themselves for their next assignments. Yet some executives take actions that subsequently backfire, setting the stage for difficulty in procuring new jobs—and even destroying their careers.

What differentiates fired employees who make the best of their situations from those who do not? One answer is mind-set. Virtually every executive feels shock and anger upon losing a job, but those who rebound swiftly have usually absorbed what we call an "assignment mentality"; they see each job as a stepping-stone, a temporary career-building project. That's good, because most corporate boards and CEOs have this mind-set, too, a continuing phenomenon that emerged about 20 years ago. Most leaders see an executive in the ranks—even the best performers—as filling an assignment. When it's over—for strategic or financial reasons—so is the executive's tenure with the company.

On an intellectual level, most executives know that the assignment mentality rules. Even so, some allow that reality to recede in their minds; it's only human nature. Then they get fired or are laid off and, like clockwork, fall into one of three traps. The first is the "lost identity" trap. Executives in this group have, over months or years, allowed themselves to "become" their jobs. Unable to imagine their companies existing without them or themselves existing without their companies, they react to termination with rage, even vengeance. The second is the "lost family" trap, the province of executives who believe that their coworkers are more than that—dear friends, even a second family. Under these circumstances, termination becomes painful estrangement, with attendant feelings of betrayal and sorrow. Finally, there is the "lost ego" trap, in which executives silently retreat from the company without negotiating fair termination packages and disappear into troughs of silent despair that make them reluctant to reach for the next opportunities.

We'll examine these traps, all of which can arise from being fired or laid off, in the following pages and then turn to a few strategies for making a dignified departure. But first, a few observations about the assignment mentality itself.

Which Mind-Set Do You Have?

The assignment model common in most companies today got its start in project-oriented industries—such as the arts, sports, agriculture, construction, and consulting. In these arenas, work comes and goes; individuals are contracted as needed; and work groups are continually assembled, altered, and dissolved. The assignment model presupposes the existence of "assignment executives"—people hired for two to six years to guide and implement a company's strategy. Sometimes, a company itself may be on assignment, in the sense that its end is foreseeable: For example, a company faced with a short product life cycle, tough competition, or an unforgiving investment community may develop a corporate exit strategy. Such an exit strategy might be to increase shareholder value by 50% and then engineer an initial public offering or an acquisition by a larger competitor. Once this strategy is successful, a new group of senior managers replaces the outgoing one.

Although the assignment model is real, it is rarely discussed. A mythic belief lives alongside it in the minds of most employees. This is the "tenure mind-set"—the comforting sense that an organization willingly parts with valued employees only when they formally retire. It has long been dead in corporate America, although most companies won't openly admit it. After all, letting employees know that their jobs are finite would make them feel disposable and would hurt recruiting efforts. For this reason, most companies perpetuate the tenure myth, particularly in corporate literature. Annual reports and other accounts, filled with glowing language about career paths, continually work to persuade employees that companies take long-term views of their career development.

Most of the time, the assignment and tenure mind-sets coexist peacefully. Externally hired CEOs truly understand that their jobs are pure assignments, because very specific termination and severance clauses are written into the employment contracts. For everyone else, the assignment nature of the job may not be clearly understood. Indeed, it's easy to ignore, even to deny. Moreover, senior executives tend to believe their own jobs are the most secure. And it isn't unusual for a founder, a CEO, or an executive promoted from within to be lulled into the tenure mind-set. When the company's exit strategy dictates a departure and sets in motion a collision between the two mind-sets, disillusionment can emerge and executives can fall into one of the three traps.

Caught in the Quagmire

When terminated suddenly, even the most widely admired and competent executives can be overcome by anger and grief. Saddled by these emotional responses, they may take actions they later regret. Let's take a closer look at these three traps.

THE LOST IDENTITY TRAP

The people most susceptible to this trap are likely to have been with a company for some time; their jobs may have been cut short due to a sudden change in course or a pressing financial crisis. Such people often include founders and senior executives who have achieved positions of power through promotion. In the day-to-day demands of doing their jobs, executives who fall into this trap have nurtured the strong sense that they are indispensable; they may have heard as much from investors or board members. Confronted with sudden job loss, they fall apart and often lash out against the former company—now rife with "enemies."

Consider Fred, a 31-year-old engineer who received his degree from MIT and then spent three years working for a large computer manufacturer. There, he developed a key technology that allowed companies to tap into their large databases via the Internet. After inventing the software, Fred decided to found a company with his own sweat equity; in time, he accepted funding from a venture capital firm with the understanding that he would be surrendering control of day-to-day operations to one of the venture partners. The partner said that Fred's continued presence was extremely important and that he hoped that Fred would consider assuming the role of chairman. Eager to finance his company, Fred agreed.

Eventually, the VC firm hired a permanent CEO, a 54-year-old man who had plenty of managerial experience but who lacked the technical skills that Fred so prized in himself. When he wanted to drive home a point, the CEO called Fred "son"; in response, Fred would mutter, "I already have a father." One day, the CEO and the VC met with Fred and fired him.

A few weeks later, Fred told us angrily, "I was kicked out of my own company." By then, Fred had done a lot of damage. In the days after his termination, he phoned each of the partners of the VC firm and accused them of betrayal. He refused to pass on his operational or engineering knowledge to anyone within the company. And when an industry analyst called to find out what had happened, Fred "secretly" confided his anger and frustration. Soon, word of Fred's unprofessional behavior circulated in both the large software industry and the small VC community. Eventually, Fred created a new start-up software company but, stamped as a person no one wanted to make deals with, was unable to secure further VC funding.

THE LOST FAMILY TRAP

This trap is most prevalent among people working in fields like marketing or magazine publishing or within start-ups—all environments of high emotional intensity. Employees in such organizations can form tight-knit, emotional bonds, just as troops in combat do. These bonds can become so close that relationships with people outside work may seem dull.

Like the main character in the 1970s sitcom *The Mary Tyler Moore Show,* executives with such intense connections can make work the emotional center of their universe. Projecting familial roles upon colleagues, who become surrogate parents, siblings, aunts, or uncles, these executives suffer grief when, on termination, the "old gang" suddenly grows distant. But who can blame the coworkers? Suffering from survivor guilt and perhaps worrying about losing their own jobs, they're instinctively turning away from the person in pain. The coworkers, too, are in shock. Executives, however, caught emotionally in the lost family trap, can't see this. They feel as if friendships have been severed and they've been rejected. As a result, they sink into bitterness and depression.

Justine was the CEO of a consumer goods manufacturing company that had once dominated its marketplace. A 15-year veteran of her company, she was an energetic workaholic who felt alive only when she was at work. Justine loved her husband and children, but she found family life mundane compared with the adrenaline-pumping game of business. Over time, however, the company began losing market share. Although the members of the board liked Justine, they felt that the company needed to go in a completely new direction by taking its manufacturing offshore; Justine fought this idea because it meant shutting down facilities and laying off beloved workers. The board, impatient to reposition the company to take advantage of new opportunities, unanimously voted to let Justine go and replace her with a new CEO.

On an intellectual level, Justine understood that anyone can be fired. As head of the company, she had arranged enough terminations to know how the game is played. But upon being fired herself, Justine believed she had lost not only her job and income but also the de facto family of which she believed herself the matriarch. When she reached out to her former subordinates, whom she had protected and befriended, they did not have time to meet her for drinks or dinner and seemed uninterested in how she was faring. The truth was that her "family" was afraid to go near her for fear that merely associating with Justine would bring them to the board's attention.

Unable to hide her depression and bitterness, Justine became an unattractive candidate. Recruiters felt she had failed to manage her board properly and hadn't rebounded from an event that should have been predictable. Unable to find work, Justine purchased a franchise retail operation, whose employees became a replacement family—and from which she could never be fired.

THE LOST EGO TRAP

Executives who fall into the lost ego trap, in our observations, tend to be introverts. Such people work very effectively in areas of the company such as accounting and finance, R&D, manufacturing, or engineering, which don't demand high levels of socialization with outside constituencies. After being unexpectedly terminated, these executives tend to withdraw.

Consider Frank, a CFO for a retail company with $50 million in sales. As a child, Frank was shy and had few friends; although he loved playing the piano, he never enjoyed public performance. After majoring in math in college, Frank earned his CPA and followed a career in finance, eventually attaining the rank of CFO. He became the acting head of the company when the CEO, after a bitter divorce, escaped on his sailboat to cruise around the world and enjoy an extended vacation on a tropical island. Although Frank was competent enough to earn the owner's trust during this long sabbatical, he was not able to prevent a loss of market share when the economy hit tough times. The fall in the company's fortunes forced the CEO to cut short his holiday; upon his return, he fired Frank and resumed control of the business with an eye toward selling it.

Although he had been with the company for 12 years, Frank reacted to the news of his termination and scant severance without a complaint and quietly left, not wanting to make a fuss. It never occurred to him to consult an attorney skilled in severance negotiations for help in procuring a more generous termination package. Every book he read on job hunting recommended networking, but he just couldn't do it; he felt that the books were telling him to be someone he wasn't. Instead of reaching out to acquaintances or taking advantage of professional networks, he relied on third parties such as recruiters or on electronic job boards to find his next position; but these efforts produced few results.

Finally, an opportunity developed with a company 150 miles away from his home. Frank listened lackadaisically as the recruiter described the position. He was already conjuring the negative aspects of the deal. "I'll have to pull the kids out of school and away from all their friends," he thought. "My wife will have to quit the job she loves. We'll have to sell our wonderful home in an uncertain housing market." Frank told the recruiter he would think about it and hung up. But rather than balancing the imagined negatives with the job's prospective benefits—the stable and growing company, a generous relocation package, the excellent position with an equity stake—Frank focused only on the downsides, which combined into an excuse to turn down the prospect without further consideration. Eventually, he accepted a far less promising position within ten miles of his house.

Exiting with Aplomb

Executives can fall into these traps—of fighting back, mourning, or fading away—when they are reacting to sudden or unexpected events. Better, of course, to be prepared, and in a moment, we'll talk about how to do that. But first, here's a piece of tactical advice. When fired or being laid off, follow the old saying and count to 100 to cool down. That is, resist the impulse to say the first thing that comes into your mind. In fact, try not to say much of anything. Contact an attorney who negotiates severance packages for senior executives. Do not call colleagues, send e-mails, or speak to reporters. In the next 48 hours, people will be contacting you. Say nothing until the severance contract has been signed. It is also important that your spouse or partner stick to whatever "official story" is being developed about you and the company.

That's the short-term fix. Now let's explore long-term strategies for departing correctly. These strategies all involve a proactive—even calculated—approach to termination. They also require adoption of the assignment mind-set: by remaining conscious of the impermanence of their jobs, executives will avoid merely reacting and can adopt systematic approaches to the next move.

Rhonda exemplifies an executive who handled her termination the right way. As a child, she had been raised to believe the adage, "If you take care of the company, the company will take care of you." After completing her MBA, she moved to San Francisco and worked at a midsized software company. When she and all her colleagues lost their jobs during an acquisition, Rhonda reevaluated her tenure mind-set. The experience persuaded her that the familiar adage was no longer tenable,

and she learned to treat successive opportunities
as moves toward her career goal of becoming a
successful CEO.

Eventually, a new e-commerce venture with a focus
on distribution hired Rhonda as its CEO. A top-tier VC
firm had proffered the first financing round of $3 million
and also promised a second round of $7 million. Rhonda—
now armed with assignment thinking—negotiated a
one-year severance package at full pay as part of the
employment contract. Soon afterward, she began growing the company, and the VC partner expressed satisfaction with her efforts. But instead of nursing illusions
of permanence, Rhonda kept a weather eye out for signs
of the company's approaching exit strategy. She likened
her assignment to "parachuting onto a sailboat during
a typhoon—I just landed with my hands on the tiller
and went from there." Aware of the perilousness of
e-commerce ventures, she cultivated her network for
the day when she would need it. She served on two corporate boards, one a computer hardware company and
the other a wireless communications company, and
spent one night every two weeks staying in touch by
phone with top business contacts. These were upbeat
conversations; she never complained to other executives
about her work.

In the spring of 2000, when the Internet bubble burst,
the VC partner announced that not only would his firm
not put in the $7 million but that it also wanted the
whole operation shut down as soon as possible. Of
course, Rhonda was angry at the partner for reneging on
his promise. But she kept her negative feelings to herself;
they passed soon enough, for she was well positioned
for the next assignment. The venture capitalist was so

impressed by Rhonda's behavior that he wrote a glowing letter of recommendation that complemented her own efforts to procure a new assignment as CEO of a new distribution company with ample financing and a strong market position.

The single most important key to Rhonda's success was her assignment mentality. Although the tenure mind-set had felt natural and comforting to her, she understood that even the most desirable job today is finite. She also understood that she was responsible for crafting her own exit strategy.

In managing current assignments and protecting options for the future, executives can follow Rhonda's example by adopting the following strategies. While not surprising or new, these tasks can be forgotten or postponed by executives too enmeshed in day-to-day work to take care of their careers. And these tactics can prove invaluable during termination.

INSERT A TERMINATION CLAUSE IN YOUR EMPLOYMENT CONTRACT

A new hire is never more attractive to the company than on the day before signing an employment contract; that's when you best control the terms of your employment. If you are newly hired or in the process of being promoted to a position that requires signing a new employment or confidentiality contract, it's possible to build your exit terms into the agreement. Like a prenuptial agreement that protects both sides if a marriage is dissolved, the insertion of such a clause at the time of hire feels completely counterintuitive. Nevertheless, it's your best hedge against a bitter exit. Hire a lawyer with experience in employment contract negotiation to insert clauses that will provide a satisfactory exit package in the event of termination.

SCHEDULE NETWORK CALLS

Make networking a discipline, not a catch-as-catch-can activity. In an assignment-driven world, keeping one's network of professional acquaintances intact is time-consuming, but it's a critical cost of doing business. The importance of networking is obvious—which may be why managers, who sometimes put their own career needs on hold, rarely think of it. Unless network calls are explicitly scheduled and rigorously carried out, they can remain mere intentions. A biweekly calendar note reminds you to get in touch with the important people in your network—especially those with their own strong networks such as valued advisers to CEOs or partners within law, consulting, or accounting firms.

RAISE YOUR VISIBILITY—BY STEALTH

Most executives understand that if they conduct personal self-branding PR campaigns, their companies will automatically fire them; the only person with official sanction to "represent" the company is likely to be the CEO. On occasion, your company's public relations team may be able to provide you with speaking engagements or bylined articles in trade publications; but such opportunities can be rare.

That's where stealth comes in. You may not be able to talk to reporters, but you can certainly raise your visibility with other professionals. You can serve on for-profit boards, at least one of which should be in an industry other than your own. This is so important that we routinely suggest adding a clause requiring board service into an employment contract. In addition to garnering useful perspectives from peers in other arenas, serving on industry boards expands the network both within and beyond one's core business—making it possible to move into new companies and industries later on. You can also play a selective and strategic leadership role in a trade association. By volunteering for externally oriented committees—such as membership, marketing, legislative affairs, or programs—you'll be able to get in front of outside constituencies while retaining a strong industry profile.

WATCH FOR EXIT SIGNS

Being terminated should not come as a surprise, but it sometimes does. Some companies provide no warning to employees about to be terminated, for fear that advance notice may result in damage to the company—from sabotage of computer systems, for example. To be as prepared as possible, pay attention to your company's culture of termination (see the insert "Auf Wiedersehen: How to Fire Right" at the end of this article). Are people severed harshly and hustled out of the building, or is the door left open for a possible return? If the former, you may want to raise your guard and take some proactive steps. Likewise, watch for how the company itself is planning to exit, because your job depends on it. Examine the position and assignment changes within the company; do position descriptions or sets of responsibilities—including your own—imply an end? If yours does, it's entirely fair to ask whether your position will continue or how it will change once this particular work is complete. It's also helpful to cultivate a strong relationship with a founder or another trusted adviser who has "seen it all before" and who can help you stay aware of prospective changes. Remember—if you think you are about to be fired, you probably are. But if you are confused by signals being given to you, consider hiring an executive coach to help you sort them out (see the insert "Do You Need an Agent?").

VOLUNTEER TO BE TERMINATED

If the company's exit strategy appears to include you, consider volunteering to be terminated before it occurs. By initiating such a discussion, you become the actor rather than the one who is acted upon. Here's what happened when Joe, the CEO of a large firm, volunteered to be laid off as his company was acquired. The terms of his existing contract allowed Joe to stay on for two years as president of the newly merged organization while the CEO of the acquiring company became chairman. But rather than waiting to be terminated after the contract expired, Joe approached the new chairman with a suggestion. Joe said that while he knew that the contract was a fair one, he fully appreciated that the acquiring company would want to run things differently. He offered to resign, provided that an excellent severance agreement could be developed. The chairman, delighted to be saved the trouble of firing Joe, was extraordinarily generous, and Joe's severance package allowed him to retire altogether.

W E DO NOT MEAN TO suggest that executives become overly wary and move from job to job or from company to company too quickly; a lot of mobility is as damaging as a little. Rather, we posit that in most cases, a degree of self-interest in one's career—as understood in its broadest, life-spanning sense—is both healthy and necessary. Executives who hold on to the tenure myth may find it difficult to assume an assignment mentality, and understandably so. It's natural to want to believe that the company for which you work so hard cares about you. But allowing yourself to be lulled into a false sense of security sets you up for shock and disappointment when you are fired or laid off.

On the corporate level, terminations are among the most predictable crises in business. When you develop an assignment mind-set, your termination becomes predictable on a personal level, too. Then even an experience as negative as being fired can turn out to be strangely empowering. It's ironic, but true: When you assume control over the way you are fired, you can gain control over your career.

Auf Wiedersehen: How To Fire Right

EVERY INDUSTRY BOASTS companies with traditions of never rehiring people who leave, regardless of how well those employees perform. But given the growth of the assignment mind-set within corporations, the unprecedented ease of movement between companies, and the difficulty of attracting excellent employees, it no longer makes sense to slam the door behind departed workers who have been solid performers. After all, such employees do not simply vanish into the night. They go to professional meetings, where they can openly discuss their exit treatment with prospective recruits. Customers, strategic partners, distributors, or acquisition candidates may hire them. And once the noncompete clauses in their employment contracts expire, they might even decide to work for a competitor.

Many companies usher employees out the door with minimal termination packages, even sending them off under a cloud of humiliation. We call these "goodbye" terminations, because they deal in finality. In one goodbye termination, a CEO who had had a disagreement with the board was fired, although the company's press release claimed he had resigned. The chairman then issued an internal memo stating that the board had forced the CEO to resign. Employees saw the ashen-faced CEO clean out his desk and depart under the gaze of the HR vice president. Not surprisingly, morale within the company dropped precipitously, and several valued employees also quit.

A much better alternative to the goodbye termination is what we call the "auf Wiedersehen" (German for "until we see you again") termination. An auf Wiedersehen departure assumes that the company will meet the departing employee again in another context and thus conducts the termination as respectfully as possible. There are several advantages to this approach. First, by making an effort to preserve the employee's dignity and goodwill, the company decreases the chance of a backlash from the employee or of a sullied reputation for its act. Second, when there is a poor fit between an individual and a company, an auf Wiedersehen exit makes it easier for the employee to leave (or even quit) without causing trauma to the company or himself.

In addition, auf Wiedersehen terminations make it possible to re-recruit top-performing alumni. This makes excellent financial sense. According to the Corporate Leadership Council, it costs 176% of base salary to recruit and train a new IT professional and 241% of base salary to recruit and train a new middle manager. When alumni are re-recruited, costs drop to almost zero because companies don't have to pay search firms, interview candidates, train employees, or get them ramped up for productivity.

By keeping accurate performance records on past employees and staying in touch with excellent alumni, companies can also reduce the possibility of mis-hire, thus saving time and money. McKinsey, for example, sponsors alumni programs such as special breakfasts and on-line directories that allow former employees to keep in touch with the company and one another. Since alumni are also shareholders, the strong alumni-shareholder base has helped attract and retain shareholders during economic downturns.

Using an auf Wiedersehen termination policy doesn't necessarily mean that companies must spend huge amounts on termination benefits; it merely requires that companies treat departing employees with the same respect when they leave as they received when they entered. Your pay policies should also be consistent. In comparisons with your competition, don't brag that you pay at the

75th percentile for new hires but at the 50th percentile for terminations. Pay policies and termination policies are two sides of one coin called "how people are treated."

Do You Need an Agent?

CONSIDER THE FOLLOWING SCENARIO: A recruiter calls you about a "fantastic" opportunity with another company, but you are too busy to give it serious attention. So you propose an alternative. "I want to give this opportunity the consideration it deserves," you say. "Given the demands of my current job, it would not be fair to my company to spend time with you. Let me give you the phone number of my agent. She understands what would be a good fit for me. My agent will do the initial screening. If the answer is yes, then we can talk in more detail. If it's no, I will be glad to refer you to others."

Tiger Woods benefits from having an agent, but a CEO? As far-fetched as it sounds, executive agents are part of a growing industry of coaches. The reason is simple. CEOs must focus their full attention on their current jobs, but in so doing, they forget to manage their careers. As a result, when assignments end, they can find themselves grasping at opportunities rather than making strategic moves.

A CEO agent helps clients with career strategy, presentation skills, image building, networking, and employment and salary negotiations. He or she also helps to screen job opportunities, even to manage money or save face in difficult situations. But is an executive agent necessary? As partners in an executive search, coaching, and outplacement firm, we can say, "Absolutely not." This kind of professional help makes little sense for extremely senior executives—CEOs like Jack Welch or Michael Dell, for example—who are very public symbols of their enterprises. Many groups within their corporations—such as the corporate public relations and investor relations departments, who keep the CEO's name in the public eye—already do some of the work of CEO agents.

Nor are CEOs who are between assignments good candidates for agents. A CEO agent manages an employed professional's long-term career; the first priority of any job candidate is to focus on securing the next assignment, and an outplacement firm would provide a sharper focus for such an individual. Outplacement services are usually provided to senior executives as part of termination packages and thus do not require personal expense.

Nevertheless, a CEO agent can play an important role, for example, in helping to negotiate the gray area of getting from one assignment to another. Eight months before the expiration of a CEO contract, a board may begin informal discussions about whether to renew the contract and may use a retained search firm to delicately explore alternatives. At the same time, a CEO's own agent can quietly explore new options. When the company and the CEO sit down to renegotiate the employment contract, both sides benefit from a clear sense of market conditions.

A CEO agent may do the legwork to manage an individual's reputation—that intangible asset that defines an executive's individual worth. One time-consuming aspect of reputation management is networking; focused on the demands of the job, an executive may lack the time to keep the network "warm." Consider Phil, a CEO with a network of 850 business contacts. He would reach out to his network only when he needed to find his next assignment; because he didn't otherwise maintain contact or contribute to committees or associations, he became known as a taker rather than as a giver. Phil commissioned a CEO agent to keep his network warm by sending quarterly personal letters, cards, and relevant articles to his contacts; Phil only signed the letters. As a result, the time he spent looking for a new position between assignments shrank from an average of six months to three.

A CEO agent can help, too, to ensure that an individual's public reputation remains strong. According to the public relations firm Burson-Marsteller, 45% of a company's reputation rests on that of its CEO. This percentage has increased almost 14% since 1997. Moreover, 95% of analysts who select stock use CEO reputation as a key decision point.

A CEO agent sometimes acts as a career coach, a person familiar with your industry and company who can serve as a trusted, impartial sounding board and work behind the scenes to help you be more effective on the job. A coach is typically an experienced businessperson who, over the years, has developed a gift for navigating business dynamics and with whom the executive develops a close, one-on-one relationship. If, for example, an executive feels she's been given a cold shoulder by someone in the organization with whom she thought she had a good relationship, a coach can help her backtrack through communications to discern possible sources of contention. Or a coach might help an executive discover ways to sell an idea to various constituents within a company, such as strategizing on how to acquire ownership of other parts of a company while the executive maintains a focus on the core aspects of his or her job.

An agent can also supply an executive with a career management infrastructure—public relations professionals to generate a visibility program, administrative staff to keep a network warm, attorneys specializing in employment contract negotiation, financial planners, and outplacement consultants. An agent might even pair an executive with a theater director to assist with an important "performance."

As with any consulting arrangement, an executive who uses an agent should proceed with caution. Here's how.

Depend on excellent references

CEO agents are difficult to find; good ones work strictly by referral. Other CEOs, or contacts in professions that use agents (sports, publishing, media), may be able to refer you to good ones. A few search firms also provide such services. Don't forget to seek help from associations such as the Young Presidents' Organization or Renaissance Executive Forums.

Ask hard questions

Before entering into a relationship with a CEO agent, hold an exploratory meeting or two during which you ask specific questions about how the agent would help manage your career for the long term. It's also important to have an open discussion about potential conflicts of interest, because the agent may know things about your company that you don't. If, for example, the agent works for a search firm that already has a relationship with your company, it's possible that the agent could be hired to find your successor. To circumvent problems, you and your agent should outline any potential conflicts of interest that either of you can imagine. And if, for any reason, the agent is not on your ethical wavelength, pass.

Understand the arrangement

Don't hire a CEO agent for a onetime transaction. Like your CPA, financial planner, or attorney, your agent is a long-term valued adviser you expect to work with over many years. He or she must be available to you 24/7 to help you with specific work-related and career management issues; it's also wise to include your agent in occasional family discussions about plans and goals. Like professional recruiters and other personal consultants, a CEO agent is hired on retainer, typically charging 5% of the executive's cash compensation, with a $15,000 minimum yearly fee.

Set realistic goals

Work together with your agent to develop six-month and one-year game plans with pragmatic goals. You want to make discernable progress in expanding your visibility, but don't expect miracles. If you are an unknown CEO from a small firm, you probably won't be sitting on the board of a *Fortune* 500 company within three months. Before the annual contract comes up for renewal, meet with your agent to evaluate the year's accomplishments.

Originally published in July 2001
Reprint 7192

Firing Back

How Great Leaders Rebound
After Career Disasters

JEFFREY A. SONNENFELD AND

ANDREW J. WARD

Executive Summary

AMONG THE TESTS OF A LEADER, few are more
challenging—and more painful—than recovering
from a career catastrophe. Most fallen leaders, in
fact, don't recover. Still, two decades of consulting
experience, scholarly research, and their own personal experiences have convinced the authors that
leaders can triumph over tragedy—if they do so
deliberately.

Great business leaders have much in common
with the great heroes of universal myth, and they
can learn to overcome profound setbacks by thinking in heroic terms. First, they must *decide whether
or not to fight back*. Either way, they must *recruit
others into their battle*. They must then take steps to
recover their heroic status, in the process proving,

both to others and to themselves, that they have the *mettle* necessary to *recover their heroic mission.*

Bernie Marcus exemplifies this process. Devastated after Sandy Sigoloff fired him from Handy Dan, Marcus decided to forgo the distraction of litigation and instead make the marketplace his battleground. Drawing from his network of carefully nurtured relationships with both close and more distant acquaintances, Marcus was able to get funding for a new venture. He proved that he had the mettle, and recovered his heroic status, by building Home Depot, whose entrepreneurial spirit embodied his heroic mission.

As Bank One's Jamie Dimon, J. Crew's Mickey Drexler, and even Jimmy Carter, Martha Stewart, and Michael Milken have shown, stunning comebacks are possible in all industries and walks of life. Whatever the cause of your predicament, it makes sense to get your story out. The alternative is likely to be long-lasting unemployment. If the facts of your dismissal cannot be made public because they are damning, then show authentic remorse. The public is often enormously forgiving when it sees genuine contrition and atonement.

AMONG THE TESTS OF A LEADER, few are more challenging—and more painful—than recovering from a career catastrophe, whether it is caused by natural disaster, illness, misconduct, slipups, or unjust conspiratorial overthrow. But real leaders don't cave in. Defeat energizes them to rejoin the fray with greater determination and vigor.

Take the case of Jamie Dimon, who was fired as president of Citigroup but now is CEO of JPMorgan Chase. Or look at Vanguard founder Jack Bogle, who was removed from his position as president of Wellington Management but then went on to create the index fund and become a leading voice for governance reform. Similarly, there's former Coca-Cola president Steve Heyer, who was surprisingly passed over for the CEO position at Coke but then was quickly named head of Starwood Hotels. Most colorful, perhaps, is Donald Trump, who recovered from two rounds of financial distress in his casino businesses and is admired today both as a hugely successful estate developer and as a producer and star of popular reality TV shows.

These stories are still the exception rather than the rule. F. Scott Fitzgerald's famous observation that there are no second acts in American lives casts an especially dark shadow over the derailed careers of business leaders. In our research—analyzing more than 450 CEO successions between 1988 and 1992 at large, publicly traded companies—we found that only 35% of ousted CEOs returned to an active executive role within two years of departure; 22% stepped back and took only advisory roles, generally counseling smaller organizations or sitting on boards. But 43% effectively ended their careers and went into retirement.

What prevents a deposed leader from coming back? Leaders who cannot recover have a tendency to blame themselves and are often tempted to dwell on the past rather than look to the future. They secretly hold themselves responsible for their career setback, whether they were or not, and get caught in a psychological web of their own making, unable to move beyond the position they no longer hold. This dynamic is usually reinforced by well-meaning colleagues, and even by family and friends, who may try to lay blame in an attempt to make sense of the chaos surrounding the disaster. Sadly, their advice can often be more damaging than helpful.

In every culture, the ability to transcend life's adversity is an essential feature of becoming a great leader. In his influential 1949 book, *The Hero with a Thousand Faces,* anthropologist Joseph Campbell showed us that the various stories of great leaders around the world, in every culture and every era, are all essentially the same story—the "hero myth." This myth is embodied in the life stages of such universal archetypes as Moses, Jesus, Muhammad, Buddha, Aeneas, Odysseus, and the Aztecs' Tezcatlipoca. Transformational leaders follow a path that entails a call to greatness, early successes (involving tough choices), ongoing trials, profound setbacks, and, ultimately, triumph as they reintegrate into society. If Campbell were writing today, he might want to include business leaders in his study, as they must confront similar trials on their way to greatness.

This article is intended to help leaders—or anyone suffering from an unexpected setback—examine their often abrupt fall from grace and to give them a process through which they can recover, and even exceed their past accomplishments. From our 22 years of interviews with 300 fired CEOs and other derailed professionals, our scholarly study of leadership, our consulting assignments, and our own searing personal experiences, we are convinced that leaders can triumph over tragedy, provided they take conscious steps to do so. For a start, they must carefully *decide how to fight back.* Once this crucial decision has been taken, they must *recruit others into battle.* They must then *take steps to recover their heroic status,* in the process proving to themselves and others that they have the *mettle* necessary to *rediscover their heroic mission.*

Few people exemplify this journey better than President Jimmy Carter. After his devastating 1980 reelection loss to Ronald Reagan, Carter was emotionally fatigued. As he told us sometime later, "I returned to Plains, Georgia, completely exhausted, slept for almost 24 hours, and then awoke to an altogether new, unwanted, and potentially empty life." While proud of his achievements—his success in deregulating energy, for example, his efforts to promote global human rights, and his ability to broker peace between Israel and Egypt through the Camp David Accords—postelection, Carter needed to move past his sense of frustration and rejection, particularly his failure to secure the timely release of the American hostages in Iran.

Despite his pain and humiliation, Carter did not retreat into anger or self-pity. He realized that his global prominence gave him a forum to fight to restore his influential role in world events. Accordingly, he recruited others into battle by enlisting the enthusiastic support of his wife, Rosalynn; several members of his administration; academic researchers in the sciences and social sciences; world leaders; and financial backers to build the Carter Center. He proved his mettle by refusing to remove himself from the fray. Indeed, he continued to involve himself in international conflict mediation in Ethiopia and Eritrea, Liberia, Haiti, Bosnia, and Venezuela, demonstrating in the process that he was not a has-been. He regained his heroic stature when he was awarded the Nobel Peace Prize in 2002 "for his decades of untiring effort to find peaceful solutions to international conflicts, to advance democracy and human rights, and to promote economic and social development." And he has rediscovered his heroic mission by using the Carter Center to continue his drive to advance human rights and alleviate needless suffering.

Let us look now at how some great business leaders have followed the same path to recover from their own disastrous career setbacks.

Decide How to Fight Back

The first decision you will face in responding to a career disaster is the question of whether to confront the situation that brought you down—with an exhausting, expensive, and perhaps embarrassing battle—or to try to put it behind you as quickly as possible, in the hope that no one will notice or remember for long. In some cases, it's best to avoid direct and immediate confrontation. Home Depot cofounder Bernie Marcus, for example, decided to sidestep the quicksand of litigation against Sandy Sigoloff, the conglomerateur who fired Marcus from Handy Dan Home Improvement. Marcus made his battleground the marketplace rather than the courtroom. Thanks to this strategy, he was free to set the historic course for the Home Depot, which now under his successor is approaching $100 billion in sales, with several hundred thousand employees.

Other comeback kids also began with a graceful retreat. Jamie Dimon was sacked as president of Citigroup by then chairman Sandy Weill following 16 years of partnership in building the institution. When he spoke to us and to others, he did not dwell on his disappointment or sense of injustice. Monica Langley in her 2003 book *Tearing Down the Walls* describes what happened when Weill asked Dimon to resign. Dimon was shocked but replied, "You've obviously thought this through, and there's nothing I can do." As he scanned the already-prepared press release, Dimon saw that the board agreed with Weill. The firm offered Dimon a generous, nonrestrictive severance package, so a battle with Weill seemed pointless.

While he was unemployed, Dimon read biographies of great national leaders who had truly suffered. He also took up boxing—another way, perhaps, of dealing with the stress and pain. After a year of this, Dimon decided he needed closure, so he invited Weill to lunch at the Four Seasons to thank him. As Dimon recounts in Harvey Mackay's 2004 book, *We Got Fired!*: "I had mellowed by then. Sandy wasn't going to call me. . . . I knew I was ready to say thank you for what he did for me. I also knew he and I should talk about what happened. I wanted to get this event behind me so I could move on. Part of me said I had spent sixteen years with him. Twelve or thirteen were pretty good. You can't just look at one side and not the other. I made my own mistakes; I acknowledged I was partly to blame. Whether I was 40 percent or 60 percent to blame really didn't matter. I felt very good about my meeting with him." In this way, Dimon was able to turn his ouster into an event that yielded both helpful perspective and reassuring resolution.

About six months after that lunch, in March 2000, Dimon became CEO of Bank One, a huge Chicago bank that survived the merger of First Chicago and the original Banc One. That year, Bank One posted a loss of $511 million. Three years later, under Dimon's leadership, Bank One was earning record profits of $3.5 billion, and its stock price had soared 85%. Adding to the sweetness of vindication, the following year Bank One merged with JPMorgan Chase, an institution with which Weill had long wanted Citigroup to merge. Dimon became CEO of the new company and is now widely regarded as one of the most influential financial executives in the world.

Of course, it's not always a good decision to sit on the sidelines and presume that justice will prevail. The highly respected Nick Nicholas, outmaneuvered as CEO of Time Warner by his skilled rival Gerald Levin, never challenged his old firm. He went off to Vail to ski at the time, awaiting a call back to service, soon becoming a very successful investor in new businesses, a professor, and a board director. But he never regained his role as the leader of a great public enterprise. Other deposed CEOs, such as Ford's Jacques Nasser, Hewlett-Packard's Carly Fiorina, IBM's John Akers, United Air Lines' Richard Ferris, and Apple's John Sculley have similarly failed to return to lead major public firms. They were considered brilliant leaders by many and were never accused of plundering the shareholders' wealth, like some rogue CEOs of recent years. But they never fought back, and they disappeared from the corner office.

The key determinant in the fight-or-flight question is the damage (or potential damage) incurred to the leader's reputation—the most important resource of all leaders. While departed CEOs and other leaders may have enough other resources and experience to rebound, it is their reputation that will make the difference between successful career recovery and failure.

Fights that will result only in a Pyrrhic victory are best avoided. Battles of pure revenge can resemble Shakespearean tragedies, where all parties lose. Hewlett-Packard board member Tom Perkins, for example, in trying to defend his friend and fellow director George Keyworth from allegations of leaking confidential board discussions, not only brought down HP chairman

Patricia Dunn but also caused his friend far greater humiliation, forcing him off the board as well. A leader must consider whether fighting the allegations will exacerbate the damage by making the accusations more public.

When, however, the allegations are not only sufficient to cause a catastrophic career setback but would also block a career comeback, then leaders need to fight back. Consider former Israeli prime minister Ariel Sharon. He was a triumphant commander on the Egyptian front in the Six Day War of 1967. Fifteen years later, as minister of defense, Sharon initiated an attack on the Palestine Liberation Organization in Lebanon. Christian militias seized the opportunity to massacre hundreds of Palestinians in acts of revenge against the PLO in the Israeli-controlled Sabra and Shatila refugee camps.

In a February 21, 1983, cover story, *Time* magazine reported that these massacres were the result of a plot between Sharon and the militias to avenge the killing of Lebanon's Christian president Bashir Gemayel. Sharon sued *Time* in Israel and in New York in lengthy litigation. In both places, juries found *Time*'s accusations to be false and defamatory. The magazine settled and apologized. "It was a very long and hard struggle and was worth it," Sharon said publically at the time. "I came here to prove that *Time* magazine lied: We were able to prove that *Time* did lie."

A ferocious warrior, Sharon took on this carefully calculated battle for his reputation and executed it with focus and determination. He knew that if he did not vigorously defend himself, no one else would be able to help him. Sharon could not have regained his honor and returned to public office if he had not challenged these false charges and then moved on with his life.

Recruit Others into Battle

Whether you fight or tactically retreat for a while, it is essential to engage others right from the start to join your battle to put your career back on track.

Friends and acquaintances play an instrumental role in providing support and advice in the process of recovery. Those who really care for you can help you gain perspective on the good and bad choices you have made. You are also more likely to make yourself vulnerable with those you trust. Without such vulnerability, you cannot hope to achieve the candid, self-critical perspective you will need to learn from your experience. Still, although family and friends can provide invaluable personal support, they may be less effective when it comes to practical career assistance. Research has shown that slight acquaintances are actually more helpful than close friends in steering you toward opportunities for new positions in other organizations.

In an acclaimed study, Stanford University's Mark Granovetter discovered that of those individuals who landed jobs through personal contacts, only 16.7% found them through people they saw at least twice a week; 55.6% found positions through acquaintances seen at least once a year. But 27.8% of job candidates found work through distant acquaintances, whom they saw less than once a year—old college friends, former workmates, or people known through professional associations. In other words, more job contacts will come to you through people you see less than once a year than from people you see twice or more a week. That's because close friends share the same networks as you do, whereas acquaintances are more likely to introduce you to new people and contacts. Indeed, through the power of acquaintance networks, you can reach almost anyone within a few steps. Thus, distant acquaintances that don't appear to have any connection to you may prove key to your recovery when you are trying to get back on your feet.

But it's not enough to have a wide network of acquaintances. The quality of the connections, even the more distant ones, matters as well. That was the case for Home Depot's Bernie Marcus. Marcus was devastated when he was fired as CEO of Handy Dan on what he felt were trumped-up charges made by Sandy Sigoloff, the threatened boss of the parent company, Daylin. "There was a lot of self-pity on my part," Marcus told us. "I was drowning in my sorrow, going several nights at a time without sleeping. For the first time in my adult life, instead of building, I was more concerned with surviving."

Marcus, however, had an unexpected resource. Whether they were close friends and colleagues with whom he worked or acquaintances he dealt with on a casual basis, Marcus treated others with uncommon honesty, respect, and trust. This consideration was recip-rocated by people in his network when he needed help; it was one of his less frequent acquaintances, Rip Fleming at Security Pacific National Bank, who made it possible for Marcus to launch Home Depot.

Marcus had raised $2 million in seed money for the Home Depot venture, but this was not enough to get his new company off the ground. He applied to several banks for a line of credit but was turned down every time. Eventually, he knocked at Fleming's door at Security Pacific National. Both Marcus and Fleming believed that the relationship between banker and client should amount to more than just the business transactions they conducted. Consequently, Fleming had become an adviser to Marcus at Handy Dan. Despite these strong professional ties, though, Fleming was initially reluctant to issue a line of credit until Marcus flew out to Los Angeles and sold Fleming on the idea. In the end, Security Pacific National provided a $3.5 million line of credit, which enabled Home Depot to get up and running. Unbeknownst to Marcus, the proposal was repeatedly turned down by the bank's loan committee and was approved only when Fleming marched into the president's office with his resignation letter in hand.

How you build relationships has a huge impact on your prospects for career recovery. Marcus had a way of building relatively strong relationships even in circumstances when most people would settle for weak acquaintanceships. This capacity for affiliation is a litmus test of a leader's ability to bounce back. People who can create connections are much more likely to engender the kind of help they need when fate turns against them.

Recover Your Heroic Status

It's not enough for you to recruit others to advance your career. To launch your comeback, you must actually *do* things to win back the support of a wider audience. To manage this, you must regain what we call your heroic status.

The great leader has a heroic persona that confers a larger-than-life presence. You can achieve this status by developing a personal dream that you offer as a public possession. If your dream is accepted, you achieve renown. If for whatever reason your public vision is ultimately discarded, you suffer the loss of both your private dream and your public identity. After a career disaster, you can rebound only if you are able to rebuild your heroic stature—that is, the public reputation with which you were previously perceived. An intrinsic part of recovering this heroic status involves getting your story out. This calls for a public campaign to educate and inform.

When a CEO is fired, the true causes for the dismissal are often deliberately hidden, as the board seeks to protect the reputation of the firm and itself. The organization often engages in elaborate face-saving activities to disguise the real nature of the exit. Euphemistically, the press reports that the CEO resigned "for personal reasons" or "to spend more time with family." In our interviews with dismissed CEOs, we found that their greatest frustration stemmed from not being able to rebuild their heroic stature by telling their side of the story. We have interviewed several people who had seven-figure separation agreements that were contingent on their toeing the party line when they left. That's a problem when CEOs are publicly sacrificed even though they are not guilty of the accusations that led to their ouster. In such cases, CEOs' inability to challenge and set the record straight can lead to destructive speculation in the press, which can damage their reputations so much that it becomes all but impossible to recover.

Popular wisdom holds that a deposed leader should sign the nondisparagement agreement, accept the noncompete clause, take the money, and run. Our strong belief is that such agreements are a mistake. In the end, your cash will disappear, and you won't be able to get your story out. If you agree not to speak out, be prepared to be unemployed for a number of years.

A lesser-known player in the Enron saga, Daniel Scotto, comes to mind. Scotto was the financial analyst who headed up the research department for the large global investment bank Paribas. Early on, Scotto said that Enron was losing money in all its mainstream businesses and that it was only through offshore finagling that the company was creating the image of profitability. Paribas, which was underwriting a large part of the debt, asked Scotto to recant. When he wouldn't, Paribas put him on an imposed medical leave for three weeks and then fired him. He was forced to sign a non-disparagement agreement that hurt his ability to get his story out. Scotto has been unemployed for five years.

Martha Stewart is the best reminder that it doesn't have to be that way. As the most public example in recent times of a CEO who got her story out, Stewart is a model for how to regain your heroic status. She did it by carefully orchestrating a multitiered campaign to restore her reputation.

The day after she was indicted for obstruction of justice in the federal government's insider-trading investigation of ImClone stock, Stewart took out a full-page advertisement in *USA Today* and the *New York Times,* and launched a new Web site, marthatalks.com. In an open letter to her public, Stewart clearly proclaimed her innocence and her intention to clear her name. She understood intuitively that when a hero stumbles, constituents have to reconcile two conflicting images of the person—the larger-than-life presence the hero once commanded and the hero's new fallen state. In her letter, Stewart managed to eliminate the confusion by making sure that people knew her side of the story. She openly denied any charges of insider trading and hammered home the unreliability of the three witnesses upon which the government based its case. Stewart very proactively helped others continue to believe in her heroic status.

Stewart's open letter was supported by a statement on her Web site by her attorneys, Robert G. Morvillo and

John J. Tigue, Jr., who challenged the media to investigate why the government waited nearly a year and a half to file the charges. "Is it because she is a woman who has successfully competed in a man's business world by virtue of her talent, hard work, and demanding standards?" they asked.

With the aid of her attorneys, Stewart ingeniously— and successfully—portrayed herself as a David struggling in a just and valiant quest against the Goliath of government. Her fans, far from abandoning a fallen star, rallied around her. The astounding strength of this sentiment is measured in the stock price of Martha Stewart Living Omnimedia. Even at the midpoint of Stewart's prison sentence, the stock had not merely rebounded—it was 50% higher than before anybody had heard of ImClone and the ill-fated stock transaction. Upon her release from prison, the share price neared an all-time high, ad revenue at her magazines picked up, and she launched two national network TV shows. The more Stewart got her story out, the more loyal her public became.

Stewart managed to provide a reassuring account of what really happened in her case. But what if you can't? What if you have truly stumbled? If you cannot refute the facts of your dismissal because they are so condemning, show authentic remorse. The public is often enormously forgiving of genuine contrition and atonement.

Prove Your Mettle

Protecting your reputation by knowing how to fight unjust accusations and bringing others on board are both essential precursors to relaunching a career in the aftermath of catastrophe. Ultimately, however, you will recover fully only when you take on that next role or start a new organization. When you show that you can still perform at a credible or superior level, others will begin to think of you as having the mettle to triumph over your career calamity.

Showing mettle is not easy. Fallen leaders face many barriers on the path to recovery, not least of which are doubts in their own ability to get back to the top. As one fired CEO told us, "I'd never sit here and say, 'Geez, all I have to do is just replicate and do it again.' The chances of doing it again are pretty small." Yet leaders who rebound are unfailingly those who get over this doubt about their ability to do it again. Even when forced from familiar arenas into totally new fields, some leaders remain un-afraid of trying new ventures. This capacity to bounce back from adversity—to prove your inner strength once more by overcoming your shattered confidence—is critical to earning lasting greatness.

Take Mickey Drexler. When Gap founder Donald Fisher poached Drexler away from Ann Taylor in 1983, the Gap was struggling to compete, since it sold the same brands of clothing as everyone else and was caught in a pricing game. Drexler expanded the retailer beyond the core Gap stores to brand extension such as GapKids, babyGap, and Gap-Body, as well as introducing other complementary brands, including Banana Republic and Old Navy. Between the time he arrived in 1983 and 2000, Gap's sales increased from $480 million to $13.7 billion, and its stock rose 169-fold.

Then things began to go awry. Drexler was accused of having lost his touch as a prescient merchant; suspicion arose in the minds of analysts and in the media that the goods had become too trendy. Although some people have suggested that the real problem was that Fisher's brother had built too many stores too close to one another, Drexler was blamed for the slump, as same-store sales dropped every quarter for two years, and the stock plummeted 75%. On May 21, 2002, Drexler presented the upcoming season's merchandise to the board, confident that he had a great selling line for the fall. It wasn't enough for the directors, and the next morning Fisher fired him, believing that the company was now too large for Drexler's hands-on management style.

Drexler was by this time independently wealthy, but he was nonetheless determined to prove that the failures of the previous two years were not primarily his fault and did not reflect his abilities. He knew that the only way to restore his belief in himself, as well as other people's confidence in him, was to return to a role in which he could once again demonstrate his expertise. He turned down a multimillion-dollar severance package from Gap because it contained a noncompete clause. After he explored a few other avenues, opportunity came knocking in the guise of struggling fashion retailer J. Crew.

With only about 200 stores, J. Crew was a small fraction of the Gap's size and consequently much more amenable to Drexler's hands-on style, giving him a greater opportunity to make an impact. Drexler invested $10 million of his own money to buy a 22% stake in the company from the retailer's private owner, the investment firm Texas Pacific. He took a salary that was less than a tenth of what he had earned at his former employer. "You've no idea how much it's costing me to run this company," he joked in a *New York* magazine article shortly after taking over.

The results more than proved that Drexler still had the right stuff. J. Crew rebounded from a $30 million operating loss in 2003 to an operating profit of over $37 million in 2004. Same-store sales per square foot, one of the key metrics in retailing, rose 18% from $338 to $400, while at his old employer, sales per square foot dropped 3%. By the summer of 2006, Drexler had increased both sales and profits 20% and launched a wildly embraced IPO to take J. Crew public. The media celebrated his recovery and acknowledged his obvious talent.

For Drexler, as for others, the comeback required him to prove his worth in a situation that was perceived to be enormously difficult. Start-ups or turnarounds are common contexts in which fallen leaders can recover grace. It is in these demanding situations that leaders find the mettle to prove to themselves and to others that they have not lost their magic touch and that no obstacle is too great to overcome in their quest for return.

Rediscover Your Heroic Mission

Most great leaders want to build a legacy that will last beyond their lifetime. This does not mean having their names etched on an ivy-clad university ediface but rather advancing society by building and leading an organization. This is what we call the leader's heroic mission.

Most of the leaders we have profiled in this article were deeply engaged in building a lasting legacy even before they suffered their career setbacks. It is the loss of this mission that really raises a derailment to catastrophic proportions in the leader's own mind, since it puts at risk a lifetime of achievement. On the day Steve Jobs was fired from Apple in 1985, for example, his friend Mike Murray was so concerned about Jobs' reaction that he went over to Jobs' house and sat with him for hours until Murray was convinced that Jobs would not commit suicide.

Jobs did not wallow in despair for long. A week after his ouster from Apple, he flew to Europe and, after a few days in Paris, headed for the Tuscan hills of northern Italy, where he bought a bicycle and a sleeping bag and camped out under the stars, contemplating what he would do next. From Italy, he went to Sweden and then to Russia before returning home. Once back in California, with his passion and ambition renewed, Jobs set about recreating himself as a force in the IT world. He went on to found another computer company, NeXT, which Apple purchased in 1996 for $400 million, at which point Jobs returned to Apple and at the same time became the driving force behind the hugely successful computer-graphics studio Pixar. Once back at Apple, Jobs revived and reenergized the company with break-through, high-design products, such as the iMac, iBook, and iPod and took the company into emerging businesses, such as iTunes.

Like Martha Stewart, Steve Jobs was able to recapture his original heroic mission. Other deposed leaders, however, must truly start again because the door to their familiar field is firmly closed, and they must seek new opportunities and create a totally new heroic mission.

That's what Drexel Burnham Lambert financier Michael Milken, the imaginative "king of the junk bonds," had to do. Milken's life was almost the incarnation of the American dream. Born on the Fourth of July, Milken had become a billionaire by his mid-forties and one of the most influential financiers in the world. Then it all came tumbling down. He was charged with a 98-count criminal indictment, and a massive civil case was brought against him by the SEC for insider trading, stock parking, price manipulation, racketeering, and defrauding customers, among other crimes. He ended up pleading guilty to six relatively minor counts. In November 1990, he was sentenced to ten years in prison, agreed to pay $600 million at the time, and ended up paying a further $42 million over a probation violation. After serving 22 months, Milken was released early for cooperating with other inquiries. But he was barred from the securities industry for life.

A week later, Milken was diagnosed with prostate cancer and was told he had 12 to 18 months to live. He immediately turned his maniacal zeal into a new heroic mission to conquer this disease. Through aggressive treatment and his own dietary research, he survived to build a huge foundation supporting research to battle prostate cancer. He also created an economic research institute that attracts the world's top scientific, political, religious, and business leaders. Milken still argues that he was wrongly accused. Others may disagree, but few would doubt that he has earned restitution. The public has come to accept that he has paid for his crimes, and there has even been some reconsideration of their actual severity.

It is the single-minded, passionate pursuit of a heroic mission that sets leaders like Steve Jobs and Michael Milken and Jimmy Carter apart from the general population, and it is what attracts and motivates followers to join them. In the worst of cases, to have that life purpose ripped from you and to be prohibited from its further pursuit can leave an unbearable void and doubts as to your reason for being. Finding a new mission to replace your lifelong purpose can be a great struggle, but one that is necessary if you are to recover.

T HE TRAGEDIES and triumphant comebacks of the leaders we have profiled in this article can seem remote, bordering on the mythological, perhaps. But their stories point to important lessons about recovering from career catastrophe. Stunning comeback is possible in all industries, though the challenges vary according to the leadership norms of each field's culture. For example, clergy ensnarled in publicized sex scandals will probably see their careers dissolve, whereas entertainment figures may not only recover but actually benefit from notoriety. Where one profession values trust, another values celebrity. Thus, recovery plans must be adapted to the cultures of different industries.

Whatever the arena in which your recovery takes shape, the important thing to remember is that we all have choices in life, even in defeat. We can lose our health, our loved ones, our jobs, but much can be saved. No one can truly define success and failure for us—only we can define that for ourselves. No one can take away our dignity unless we surrender it. No one can take away our hope and pride unless we relinquish them. No one can steal our creativity, imagination, and skills unless we stop thinking. No one can stop us from rebounding unless we give up.

Getting Beyond Rage and Denial

ONE OF THE MOST important steps on the route to recovery is to confront and acknowledge failure. This can be as simple as understanding the Machiavellian politics of others. So as you set about rebuilding your career, make sure you:

- **Remember that failure is a beginning, not an end.** Comeback is always possible.

- **Look to the future.** Preemptive actions are often more effective than reactive ones—even if they only take the form of standing back and reflecting on what to do next.

- **Help people to deal with your failure.** Even close friends may avoid you because they don't know what to say or do. Let them know that you are ready for assistance and what kind of aid would be most useful.

- **Know your narrative.** Reputation building involves telling and retelling your story to get your account of events out there and to explain your downfall. Be consistent.

How to Come Back

OUR INTERVIEWS with some 300 derailed CEOs and other professionals, as well as our scholarly leadership research, consulting assignments, and personal experiences, have brought to light five key steps for rebounding from career disaster. Anyone trying to recover from a catastrophic setback can use these steps to match, or even exceed, their past accomplishments:

- **Decide how to fight back.** Pyrrhic victories will hurt you by calling attention to the accusations leveled against you. But when your reputation is unfairly damaged, you must take quick action.

- **Recruit others into battle.** Friends and family can provide comfort and, perhaps, some perspective in your hour of need. But acquaintances may be more important in landing that next job.

- **Recover your heroic status.** Deposed leaders are often advised to sign nondisparagement agreements. Don't do it. Engage instead in a multitiered campaign to clear your reputation and restore your stature.

- **Prove your mettle.** After suffering career disaster, you will probably have doubts about your ability to get back to the top. You must overcome that insecurity and in the process find the courage to prove to others—and yourself—that you have not lost your magic touch.

- **Rediscover your heroic mission.** It is the single-minded pursuit of a lasting legacy that sets great leaders apart. To recover from a disastrous setback, find a new heroic mission that renews your passion and creates new meaning in your life.

Originally published in January 2007
Reprint R0701G

How Resilience Works

DIANE L. COUTU

Executive Summary

WHY DO SOME PEOPLE bounce back from life's hardships while others despair? HBR senior editor Diane Coutu looks at the nature of individual and organizational resilience, issues that have gained special urgency in light of the recent terrorist attacks, war, and recession. In the business arena, resilience has found its way onto the list of qualities sought in employees. As one of Coutu's interviewees puts it, "More than education, more than experience, more than training, a person's level of resilience will determine who succeeds and who fails."

Theories abound about what produces resilience, but three fundamental characteristics seem to set resilient people and companies apart from others. One or two of these qualities make it possible to bounce back from hardship, but true resilience requires all three.

The first characteristic is the capacity to accept and face down reality. In looking hard at reality, we prepare ourselves to act in ways that allow us to endure and survive hardships: We train ourselves how to survive before we ever have to do so.

Second, resilient people and organizations possess an ability to find meaning in some aspects of life. And values are just as important as meaning; value systems at resilient companies change very little over the long haul and are used as scaffolding in times of trouble.

The third building block of resilience is the ability to improvise. Within an arena of personal capabilities or company rules, the ability to solve problems without the usual or obvious tools is a great strength.

W HEN I BEGAN MY CAREER in journalism—I was a reporter at a national magazine in those days—there was a man I'll call Claus Schmidt. He was in his mid-fifties, and to my impressionable eyes, he was the quintessential newsman: cynical at times, but unrelentingly curious and full of life, and often hilariously funny in a sandpaper-dry kind of way. He churned out hard-hitting cover stories and features with a speed and elegance I could only dream of. It always astounded me that he was never promoted to managing editor.

But people who knew Claus better than I did thought of him not just as a great newsman but as a quintessential survivor, someone who had endured in an environment often hostile to talent. He had lived through at least three major changes in the magazine's leadership, losing most of his best friends and colleagues on the way. At home, two of his children succumbed to incurable illnesses, and a third was killed in a traffic accident. Despite all this—or maybe because of it—he milled around the newsroom day after day, mentoring the cub reporters, talking about the novels he was writing— always looking forward to what the future held for him.

Why do some people suffer real hardships and not falter? Claus Schmidt could have reacted very differently. We've all seen that happen: One person cannot seem to get the confidence back after a layoff; another, persistently depressed, takes a few years off from life after her divorce. The question we would all like answered is, Why? What exactly is that quality of resilience that carries people through life?

It's a question that has fascinated me ever since I first learned of the Holocaust survivors in elementary school. In college, and later in my studies as an affiliate scholar at the Boston Psychoanalytic Society and Institute, I returned to the subject. For the past several months, however, I have looked on it with a new urgency, for it seems to me that the terrorism, war, and recession of recent months have made understanding resilience more important than ever. I have considered both the nature of individual resilience and what makes some organizations as a whole more resilient than others. Why do some people and some companies buckle under pressure? And what makes others bend and ultimately bounce back?

My exploration has taught me much about resilience, although it's a subject none of us will ever understand fully. Indeed, resilience is one of the great puzzles of human nature, like creativity or the religious instinct. But in sifting through psychological research and in reflecting on the many stories of resilience I've heard, I have seen a little more deeply into the hearts and minds of people like Claus Schmidt and, in doing so, looked more deeply into the human psyche as well.

The Buzz About Resilience

Resilience is a hot topic in business these days. Not long ago, I was talking to a senior partner at a respected consulting firm about how to land the very best MBAs—the name of the game in that particular industry. The partner, Daniel Savageau (not his real name), ticked off a long list of qualities his firm sought in its hires: intelligence, ambition, integrity, analytic ability, and so on. "What about resilience?" I asked. "Well, that's very popular right now," he said. "It's the new buzzword. Candidates even tell us they're resilient; they volunteer the information. But frankly, they're just too young to know that about themselves. Resilience is something you realize you have *after* the fact."

"But if you could, would you test for it?" I asked. "Does it matter in business?"

Savageau paused. He's a man in his late forties and a success personally and professionally. Yet it hadn't been a smooth ride to the top. He'd started his life as a poor French Canadian in Woonsocket, Rhode Island, and had lost his father at six. He lucked into a football scholarship but was kicked out of Boston University twice for drinking. He turned his life around in his twenties, married, divorced, remarried, and raised five children. Along the way, he made and lost two fortunes before helping to found the consulting firm he now runs. "Yes, it does matter," he said at last. "In fact, it probably matters more than any of the usual things we look for." In the course of reporting this article, I heard the same assertion time and again. As Dean Becker, the president and CEO of Adaptiv Learning Systems, a four-year-old company in King of Prussia, Pennsylvania, that develops and delivers programs about resilience training, puts it: "More than education, more than experience, more than training, a person's level of resilience will determine who succeeds and who fails. That's true in the cancer ward, it's true in the Olympics, and it's true in the boardroom."

Academic research into resilience started about 40 years ago with pioneering studies by Norman Garmezy, now a professor emeritus at the University of Minnesota in Minneapolis. After studying why many children of schizophrenic parents did not suffer psychological illness as a result of growing up with them, he concluded that a certain quality of resilience played a greater role in mental health than anyone had previously suspected.

Today, theories abound about what makes resilience. Looking at Holocaust victims, Maurice Vanderpol, a former president of the Boston Psychoanalytic Society and Institute, found that many of the healthy survivors of concentration camps had what he calls a "plastic shield." The shield was comprised of several factors, including a sense of humor. Often the humor was black, but nonetheless it provided a critical sense of perspective. Other core characteristics that helped included the ability to form attachments to others and the possession of an inner psychological space that protected the survivors from the intrusions of abusive others. Research about other groups uncovered different qualities associated with resilience. The Search Institute, a Minneapolis-based nonprofit organization that focuses on resilience and youth, found that the more resilient kids have an uncanny ability to get adults to help them out. Still other research showed that resilient inner-city youth often have talents such as athletic abilities that attract others to them.

Many of the early theories about resilience stressed the role of genetics. Some people are just born resilient, so the arguments went. There's some truth to that, of course, but an increasing body of empirical evidence shows that resilience—whether in children, survivors of concentration camps, or businesses back from the brink—can be learned. For example, George Vaillant, the director of the Study of Adult Development at Harvard Medical School in Boston, observes that within various groups studied during a 60-year period, some people became markedly more resilient over their lifetimes. Other psychologists claim that unresilient people more easily develop resiliency skills than those with head starts.

Most of the resilience theories I encountered in my research make good common sense. But I also observed that almost all the theories overlap in three ways. Resilient people, they posit, possess three characteristics: a staunch acceptance of reality; a deep belief, often buttressed by strongly held values, that life is meaningful; and an uncanny ability to improvise. You can bounce back from hardship with just one or two of these qualities, but you will only be truly resilient with all three. These three characteristics hold true for resilient organizations as well. Let's take a look at each of them in turn.

Facing Down Reality

A common belief about resilience is that it stems from an optimistic nature. That's true but only as long as such optimism doesn't distort your sense of reality. In extremely adverse situations, rose-colored thinking can actually spell disaster. This point was made poignantly to me by management researcher and writer Jim Collins, who happened upon this concept while researching *Good to Great*, his book on how companies transform themselves out of mediocrity. Collins had a hunch (an exactly wrong hunch) that resilient companies were filled with optimistic people. He tried out that idea on Admiral Jim Stockdale, who was held prisoner and tortured by the Vietcong for eight years.

Collins recalls: "I asked Stockdale: 'Who didn't make it out of the camps?' And he said, 'Oh, that's easy. It was the optimists. They were the ones who said we were going to be out by Christmas. And then they said we'd be out by Easter and then out by Fourth of July and out by Thanksgiving, and then it was Christmas again.' Then Stockdale turned to me and said, 'You know, I think they all died of broken hearts.'"

In the business world, Collins found the same unblinking attitude shared by executives at all the most successful companies he studied. Like Stockdale, resilient people have very sober and down-to-earth views of those parts of reality that matter for survival. That's not to say that optimism doesn't have its place: In turning around a demoralized sales force, for instance, conjuring a sense of possibility can be a very powerful tool. But for bigger challenges, a cool, almost pessimistic, sense of reality is far more important.

Perhaps you're asking yourself, "Do I truly understand—and accept—the reality of my situation? Does my organization?" Those are good questions, particularly because research suggests most people slip into denial as a coping mechanism. Facing reality, really facing it, is grueling work. Indeed, it can be unpleasant and often emotionally wrenching. Consider the following story of organizational resilience, and see what it means to confront reality.

Prior to September 11, 2001, Morgan Stanley, the famous investment bank, was the largest tenant in the World Trade Center. The company had some 2,700 employees working in the south tower on 22 floors between the 43rd and the 74th. On that horrible day, the first plane hit the north tower at 8:46 AM, and Morgan Stanley started evacuating just one minute later, at 8:47 AM. When the second plane crashed into the south tower 15 minutes after that, Morgan Stanley's offices were largely empty. All told, the company lost only seven employees despite receiving an almost direct hit.

Of course, the organization was just plain lucky to be in the second tower. Cantor Fitzgerald, whose offices were hit in the first attack, couldn't have done anything to save its employees. Still, it was Morgan Stanley's hard-nosed realism that enabled the company to benefit from its luck. Soon after the 1993 attack on the World Trade Center, senior management recognized that working in such a symbolic center of U.S. commercial power made the company vulnerable to attention from terrorists and possible attack.

With this grim realization, Morgan Stanley launched a program of preparedness at the micro level. Few companies take their fire drills seriously. Not so Morgan Stanley, whose VP of security for the Individual Investor Group, Rick Rescorla, brought a military discipline to the job. Rescorla, himself a highly resilient, decorated Vietnam vet, made sure that people were fully drilled about what to do in a catastrophe. When disaster struck on September 11, Rescorla was on a bullhorn telling Morgan Stanley employees to stay calm and follow their well-practiced drill, even though some building supervisors were telling occupants that all was well. Sadly, Rescorla himself, whose life story has been widely covered in recent months, was one of the seven who didn't make it out.

"When you're in financial services where so much depends on technology, contingency planning is a major part of your business," says President and COO Robert G. Scott. But Morgan Stanley was prepared for the very toughest reality. It had not just one, but three, recovery sites where employees could congregate and business could take place if work locales were ever disrupted. "Multiple backup sites seemed like an incredible extravagance on September 10," concedes Scott. "But on September 12, they seemed like genius."

Maybe it was genius; it was undoubtedly resilience at work. The fact is, when we truly stare down reality, we prepare ourselves to act in ways that allow us to endure and survive extraordinary hardship. We train ourselves how to survive before the fact.

The Search for Meaning

The ability to see reality is closely linked to the second building block of resilience, the propensity to make meaning of terrible times. We all know people who, under duress, throw up their hands and cry, "How can this be happening to me?" Such people see themselves as victims, and living through hardship carries no lessons for them. But resilient people devise constructs about their suffering to create some sort of meaning for themselves and others.

I have a friend I'll call Jackie Oiseaux who suffered repeated psychoses over a ten-year period due to an undiagnosed bipolar disorder. Today, she holds down a big job in one of the top publishing companies in the country, has a family, and is a prominent member of her church community. When people ask her how she bounced back from her crises, she runs her hands through her hair. "People sometimes say, 'Why me?' But I've always said, 'Why *not* me?' True, I lost many things during my illness," she says, "but I found many more–incredible friends who saw me through the bleakest times and who will give meaning to my life forever."

This dynamic of meaning making is, most researchers agree, the way resilient people build bridges from present-day hardships to a fuller, better constructed future. Those bridges make the present manageable, for lack of a better word, removing the sense that the present is overwhelming. This concept was beautifully articulated by Viktor E. Frankl, an Austrian psychiatrist and an Auschwitz survivor. In the midst of staggering suffering, Frankl invented "meaning therapy," a humanistic therapy technique that helps individuals make the kinds of decisions that will create significance in their lives.

In his book *Man's Search for Meaning,* Frankl described the pivotal moment in the camp when he developed meaning therapy. He was on his way to work one day, worrying whether he should trade his last cigarette for a bowl of soup. He wondered how he was going to work with a new foreman whom he knew to be particularly sadistic. Suddenly, he was disgusted by just how trivial and meaningless his life had become. He realized that to survive, he had to find some purpose. Frankl did so by imagining himself giving a lecture after the war on the psychology of the concentration camp, to help outsiders understand what he had been through. Although he wasn't even sure he would survive, Frankl created some concrete goals for himself. In doing so, he succeeded in rising above the sufferings of the moment. As he put it in his book: "We must never forget that we may also find meaning in life even when confronted with a hopeless situation, when facing a fate that cannot be changed."

Frankl's theory underlies most resilience coaching in business. Indeed, I was struck by how often businesspeople referred to his work. "Resilience training—what we call hardiness—is a way for us to help people construct meaning in their everyday lives," explains Salvatore R. Maddi, a University of California, Irvine psychology professor and the director of the Hardiness Institute in Newport Beach, California. "When people realize the power of resilience training, they often say, 'Doc, is this what psychotherapy is?' But psychotherapy is for people whose lives have fallen apart badly and need repair. We see our work as showing people life skills and attitudes. Maybe those things should be taught at home, maybe they should be taught in schools, but they're not. So we end up doing it in business."

Yet the challenge confronting resilience trainers is often more difficult than we might imagine. Meaning can be elusive, and just because you found it once doesn't mean you'll keep it or find it again. Consider Aleksandr Solzhenitsyn, who survived the war against the Nazis, imprisonment in the gulag, and cancer. Yet when he moved to a farm in peaceful, safe Vermont, he could not cope with the "infantile West." He was unable to discern any real meaning in what he felt to be the destructive and irresponsible freedom of the West. Upset by his critics, he withdrew into his farmhouse, behind a locked fence, seldom to be seen in public. In 1994, a bitter man, Solzhenitsyn moved back to Russia.

Since finding meaning in one's environment is such
an important aspect of resilience, it should come as no
surprise that the most successful organizations and
people possess strong value systems. Strong values infuse
an environment with meaning because they offer ways to
interpret and shape events. While it's popular these days
to ridicule values, it's surely no coincidence that the
most resilient organization in the world has been the
Catholic Church, which has survived wars, corruption,
and schism for more than 2,000 years, thanks largely to
its immutable set of values. Businesses that survive also
have their creeds, which give them purposes beyond just
making money. Strikingly, many companies describe
their value systems in religious terms. Pharmaceutical
giant Johnson & Johnson, for instance, calls its value sys-
tem, set out in a document given to every new employee
at orientation, the Credo. Parcel company UPS talks constantly about its Noble Purpose.

Value systems at resilient companies change very little
over the years and are used as scaffolding in times of
trouble. UPS Chairman and CEO Mike Eskew believes that
the Noble Purpose helped the company to rally after the
agonizing strike in 1997. Says Eskew: "It was a hugely difficult time, like a family feud. Everyone had close friends on
both sides of the fence, and it was tough for us to pick
sides. But what saved us was our Noble Purpose. Whatever
side people were on, they all shared a common set of values. Those values are core to us and never change; they
frame most of our important decisions. Our strategy and
our mission may change, but our values never do."

The religious connotations of words like "credo,"
"values," and "noble purpose," however, should not
be confused with the actual content of the values.
Companies can hold ethically questionable values and
still be very resilient. Consider Phillip Morris, which has

demonstrated impressive resilience in the face of increasing unpopularity. As Jim Collins points out, Phillip Morris has very strong values, although we might not agree with them–for instance, the value of "adult choice." But there's no doubt that Phillip Morris executives believe strongly in its values, and the strength of their beliefs sets the company apart from most of the other tobacco companies. In this context, it is worth noting that resilience is neither ethically good nor bad. It is merely the skill and the capacity to be robust under conditions of enormous stress and change. As Viktor Frankl wrote: "On the average, only those prisoners could keep alive who, after years of trekking from camp to camp, had lost all scruples in their fight for existence; they were prepared to use every means, honest and otherwise, even brutal . . . , in order to save themselves. We who have come back . . . we know: The best of us did not return."

Values, positive or negative, are actually more important for organizational resilience than having resilient people on the payroll. If resilient employees are all interpreting reality in different ways, their decisions and actions may well conflict, calling into doubt the survival of their organization. And as the weakness of an organization becomes apparent, highly resilient individuals are more likely to jettison the organization than to imperil their own survival.

Ritualized Ingenuity

The third building block of resilience is the ability to make do with whatever is at hand. Psychologists follow the lead of French anthropologist Claude Levi-Strauss in calling this skill bricolage.[1] Intriguingly, the roots of that word are closely tied to the concept of resilience, which literally means "bouncing back." Says Levi-Strauss: "In its old sense, the verb *bricoler* . . . was always used with reference to some extraneous movement: a ball rebounding, a dog straying, or a horse swerving from its direct course to avoid an obstacle."

Bricolage in the modern sense can be defined as a kind of inventiveness, an ability to improvise a solution to a problem without proper or obvious tools or materials. *Bricoleurs* are always tinkering—building radios from household effects or fixing their own cars. They make the most of what they have, putting objects to unfamiliar uses. In the concentration camps, for example, resilient inmates knew to pocket pieces of string or wire whenever they found them. The string or wire might later become useful–to fix a pair of shoes, perhaps, which in freezing conditions might make the difference between life and death.

When situations unravel, bricoleurs muddle through, imagining possibilities where others are confounded. I have two friends, whom I'll call Paul Shields and Mike Andrews, who were roommates throughout their college years. To no one's surprise, when they graduated, they set up a business together, selling educational materials to schools, businesses, and consulting firms. At first, the company was a great success, making both founders paper millionaires. But the recession of the early 1990s hit the company hard, and many core clients fell away. At the same time, Paul experienced a bitter divorce and a depression that made it impossible for him to work. Mike offered to buy Paul out but was instead slapped with a lawsuit claiming that Mike was trying to steal the business. At this point, a less resilient person might have just walked away from the mess. Not Mike. As the case wound through the courts, he kept the company going any way he could—constantly morphing the business until he found a model that worked: going into joint ventures to sell English-language training materials to Russian and Chinese companies. Later, he branched off into publishing newsletters for clients. At one point, he was even writing video scripts for his competitors. Thanks to all this bricolage, by the time the lawsuit was settled in his favor, Mike had an entirely different, and much more solid, business than the one he had started with.

Bricolage can be practiced on a higher level as well. Richard Feynman, winner of the 1965 Nobel Prize in physics, exemplified what I like to think of as intellectual bricolage. Out of pure curiosity, Feynman made himself an expert on cracking safes, not only looking at the mechanics of safecracking but also cobbling together psychological insights about people who used safes and set the locks. He cracked many of the safes at Los Alamos, for instance, because he guessed that theoretical physicists would not set the locks with random code numbers they might forget but would instead use a sequence with mathematical significance. It turned out that the three safes containing all the secrets to the atomic bomb were set to the same mathematical constant, *e,* whose first six digits are 2.71828.

Resilient organizations are stuffed with bricoleurs, though not all of them, of course, are Richard Feynmans. Indeed, companies that survive regard improvisation as a core skill. Consider UPS, which empowers its drivers to do whatever it takes to deliver packages on time. Says CEO Eskew: "We tell our employees to get the job done. If that means they need to improvise, they improvise. Otherwise we just couldn't do what we do every day. Just think what can go wrong: a busted traffic light, a flat tire, a bridge washed out. If a snowstorm hits Louisville tonight, a group of people will sit together and discuss how to handle the problem. Nobody tells them to do that. They come together because it's our tradition to do so."

That tradition meant that the company was delivering parcels in southeast Florida just one day after Hurricane Andrew devastated the region in 1992, causing billions of dollars in damage. Many people were living in their cars because their homes had been destroyed, yet UPS drivers and managers sorted packages at a diversion site and made deliveries even to those who were stranded in their cars. It was largely UPS's improvisational skills that enabled it to keep functioning after the catastrophic hit. And the fact that the company continued on gave others a sense of purpose or meaning amid the chaos.

Improvisation of the sort practiced by UPS, however, is a far cry from unbridled creativity. Indeed, much like the military, UPS lives on rules and regulations. As Eskew says: "Drivers always put their keys in the same place. They close the doors the same way. They wear their uniforms the same way. We are a company of precision." He believes that although they may seem stifling, UPS's rules were what allowed the company to bounce back immediately after Hurricane Andrew, for they enabled people to focus on the one or two fixes they needed to make in order to keep going.

Eskew's opinion is echoed by Karl E. Weick, a professor of organizational behavior at the University of Michigan Business School in Ann Arbor and one of the most respected thinkers on organizational psychology. "There is good evidence that when people are put under pressure, they regress to their most habituated ways of responding," Weick has written. "What we do not expect under life-threatening pressure is creativity." In other words, the rules and regulations that make some companies appear less creative may actually make them more resilient in times of real turbulence.

CLAUS CHMIDT, the newsman I mentioned earlier, died about five years ago, but I'm not sure I could have interviewed him about his own resilience even if he were alive. It would have felt strange, I think, to ask him, "Claus, did you really face down reality? Did you make meaning out of your hardships? Did you improvise your recovery after each professional and personal disaster?" He may not have been able to answer. In my experience, resilient people don't often describe themselves that way. They shrug off their survival stories and very often assign them to luck.

Obviously, luck does have a lot to do with surviving. It was luck that Morgan Stanley was situated in the south tower and could put its preparedness training to work. But being lucky is not the same as being resilient. Resilience is a reflex, a way of facing and understanding the world, that is deeply etched into a person's mind and soul. Resilient people and companies face reality with staunchness, make meaning of hardship instead of crying out in despair, and improvise solutions from thin air. Others do not. This is the nature of resilience, and we will never completely understand it.

Note

1. See, e.g., Karl E. Weick, "The Collapse of Sense-making in Organizations: The Mann Gulch Disaster," *Administrative Science Quarterly*, December 1993.

Originally published in May 2002
Reprint 1709

What's Your Story?

HERMINIA IBARRA AND KENT LINEBACK

Executive Summary

WHEN YOU'RE IN THE MIDSt of a major career change, telling stories about your professional self can inspire others' belief in your character and in your capacity to take a leap and land on your feet. It also can help you believe in yourself. A narrative thread will give meaning to your career history; it will assure you that, in moving on to something new, you are not discarding everything you've worked so hard to accomplish.

Unfortunately, the authors explain in this article, most of us fail to use the power of storytelling in pursuit of our professional goals, or we do it badly. Tales of transition are especially challenging. Not knowing how to reconcile the built-in discontinuities in our work lives, we often relay just the facts. We present ourselves as safe—and dull and unremarkable.

That's not a necessary compromise. A transition story has inherent dramatic appeal. The protagonist is you, of course, and what's at stake is your career. Perhaps you've come to an event or insight that represents a point of no return. It's this kind of break with the past that will force you to discover and reveal who you really are. Discontinuity and tension are part of the experience. If these elements are missing from your career story, the tale will fall flat.

With all these twists and turns, how do you demonstrate stability and earn listeners' trust? By emphasizing continuity and causality—in other words, by showing that your past is related to the present and, from that trajectory, conveying that a solid future is in sight. If you can make your story of transition cohere, you will have gone far in convincing the listener—and reassuring yourself—that the change makes sense for you and is likely to bring success.

A<small>T A RECENT NETWORKING EVENT,</small> senior managers who'd been downsized out of high-paying corporate jobs took turns telling what they had done before and what they were looking for next. Person after person stood up and recounted a laundry list of credentials and jobs, in chronological order. Many felt compelled to begin with their first job, some even with their place of birth. The accounting was meticulous.

Most people spent their allotted two minutes (and lost the attention of those around them) before they even reached the punch line—the description of what they were seeking. Those who did leave time to wrap up tended merely to list the four or five (disparate) things they might be interested in pursuing next. In the feedback sessions that followed each round of presentations, these "fact tellers" were hard to help. The people listening couldn't readily understand how their knowledge and contacts might bear upon the teller's situation. Even worse, they didn't feel compelled to try very hard.

In our research and coaching on career reorientation, we've witnessed many people struggling to explain what they want to do next and why a change makes sense. One of us, in the context of writing a book, has studied a wide variety of major career shifts; the other has worked extensively with organizations and individuals on the use of narrative to bring about positive change. Each of us has been to enough networking events to know that the one we've described here is not unusual. But we've also seen a lot of people in the midst of significant transitions make effective use of contacts and successfully enlist supporters. What we've come to understand is that one factor more than any other makes the difference: the ability to craft a good story.

Why You Need a Story

All of us tell stories about ourselves. Stories define us. To know someone well is to know her story—the experiences that have shaped her, the trials and turning points that have tested her. When we want someone to know us, we share stories of our childhoods, our families, our school years, our first loves, the development of our political views, and so on.

Seldom is a good story so needed, though, as when a major change of professional direction is under way—when we are leaving A without yet having left it and moving toward B without yet having gotten there. In a time of such unsettling transition, telling a compelling story to coworkers, bosses, friends, or family—or strangers in a conference room—inspires belief in our motives, character, and capacity to reach the goals we've set.

Let's be clear: In urging the use of effective narrative, we're not opening the door to tall tales. By "story" we don't mean "something made up to make a bad situation look good." Rather, we're talking about accounts that are deeply true and so engaging that listeners feel they have a stake in our success. This dynamic was lacking in the event described above. Without a story, there was no context to render career facts meaningful, no promise of a third act in which achieving a goal (getting a job, for instance) would resolve the drama.

Creating and telling a story that resonates also helps us believe in ourselves. Most of us experience the transition to a new working life as a time of confusion, loss, insecurity, and uncertainty. We are scared. "Will I look back one day and think this was the best thing that ever happened?" we ask ourselves. "Or will I realize that this was the beginning of the end, that it was all downhill from here?" We oscillate between holding on to the past and embracing the future. Why? We have lost the narrative thread of our professional life. Without a compelling story that lends meaning, unity, and purpose to our lives, we feel lost and rudderless. We need a good story to reassure us that our plans make sense—that, in moving on, we are not discarding everything we have worked so hard to accomplish and selfishly putting family and livelihood at risk. It will give us motivation and help us endure frustration, suffering, and hard work.

A good story, then, is essential for making a successful transition. Yet most of us—like those at the networking event—fail to use the power of storytelling in pursuit of our cause. Or, when we do craft a story, we do it badly. In part, this may be because many of us have forgotten how to tell stories. But even the best storytellers find tales of transition challenging, with their built-in problems and tensions. Not knowing how to resolve these conflicts, we retreat to telling "just the facts."

Your Story Has Inherent Drama

At first glance, it's not obvious why stories of transition should present any problems at all. Almost by definition, they contain the stuff of good narrative. (See the insert "Key Elements of a Classic Story" at the end of this article.) The protagonist is you, of course, and what's at stake is your career. Only love, life, and death could be more important. And transition is always about a world that's changed. You've been let go, or you've somehow decided your life doesn't work anymore. Perhaps you've reached an event or insight that represents a point of no return—one that marks the end of the second act, a period of frustration and struggle. In the end, if all goes well, you resolve the tension and uncertainty and embark on a new chapter in your life or career.

Not only do transition stories have all the elements of a classic tale, but they have the most important ones in spades. Notice what moves a story along. It's change, conflict, tension, discontinuity. What hooks us in a movie or novel is the turning point, the break with the past, the fact that the world has changed in some intriguing and fascinating way that will force the protagonist to discover and reveal who he truly is. If those elements are missing, the story will be flat. It will lack what novelist John Gardner called profluence of development—the sense of moving forward, of going somewhere. Transition stories don't have this problem.

Think, for example, of the biblical story of Saint Paul's conversion. In his zeal for Jewish law, Saul had become a violent persecutor of Christians. On the road to Damascus, as the story is told in the New Testament, he was surrounded by light and struck to the ground. A voice from heaven addressed him: "Saul, Saul, why do you persecute me?" He was unable to see; after he changed his mind about Christians, he saw the light, literally. And thus, Saul became Paul, one of the principal architects of Christianity.

What could be more dramatic? Like the Saul-to-Paul saga, most after-the-fact accounts of career change include striking jolts and triggers: palpable moments when things click into place and a desirable option materializes. The scales fall from our eyes, and the right course becomes obvious—or taking the leap suddenly looks easy.

Here's how that turning point took shape for one manager, a 46-year-old information technologist named Lucy Hartman (names in the examples throughout this article have been changed). Lucy was seemingly on a course toward executive management, either at her current company or at a start-up. Being coached, however, revealed to her an attractive alternative. She began to wonder about a future as an organizational-development consultant, but she wasn't quite ready to make that change. She did move to a smaller company, where she felt she could apply everything she had learned in coaching. "By this time, it was clear that I wanted to move on to something different," she said. "But I needed to build

more confidence before taking a bigger chance on reinventing myself. So I decided to stay in the high-tech
environment, which I knew well, but also to go back to
school. I started a master's program in organizational
development, thinking it would at least make me a better
leader and hoping it would be the impetus for a real
makeover." Still, Lucy agonized for months over whether
to focus exclusively on school, convinced that it wasn't
sane to quit a job without having another one lined up.

Three incidents in quick succession made up her
mind. First, she attended a conference on organizational
change where she heard industry gurus speak and met
other people working in the field. She decided this was
clearly the community she wanted to be a part of.
Second, her firm went through an acquisition, and the
restructuring meant a new position for her, one fraught
with political jockeying. Third, as she tells it: "One day
my husband just asked me, 'Are you happy?' He said, 'If
you are, that's great. But you don't look happy. When I
ask how you are, all you ever say is that you're tired.'" His
question prompted her to quit her job and work full-time
on her master's.

Lucy's story illustrates the importance of turning
points. We need them to convince ourselves that our
story makes sense, and listeners like them because they
spin stories off in exciting new directions. They make listeners lean forward and ask the one question every effective story must elicit: "What happened next?"

The Challenge of the Transition Story

Let's return to that networking event and all the drab
stories (actually, nonstories) people told. If transition
stories, with their drama and discontinuity, lend

themselves so well to vivid telling, why did so many people merely recount the basic facts of their careers and avoid the exciting turning points? Why did most of them try to frame the changes in their lives as incremental, logical extensions of what they were doing before? Why did they fail to play up the narrative twists and turns?

To begin with, it's because they were attempting to tell the story while they were still in the middle of the second act. Look back over Lucy's story, and you'll realize that the turning points she described were not very different from incidents all of us experience daily. They assumed great significance for Lucy only because she made them do so. For most of us, turning points are like Lucy's rather than Saul's; they tend to be much more obvious in the telling than in the living. We must learn to use them to propel our stories forward.

Additionally, stories of transition present a challenge because telling them well involves baring some emotion. You have to let the listener know that something is at stake for you personally. When you're in a job interview or when you are speaking to relative strangers, that is difficult to do.

Another issue that makes life stories (particularly ones about discontinuity) problematic: Not only does a good story require us to trust the listener, but it must also inspire the listener to trust us. A story about life discontinuity raises red flags about the teller's capabilities, dependability, and predictability. Listeners wonder, "Why should I believe you can excel in a new arena when you don't have a track record to point to?" And on a deeper level, even greater suspicions lurk: "Why should I trust that you won't change your mind about this? You changed your mind before, didn't you?"

To tell a life story that emphasizes such juicy elements as transformation and discontinuity is to invite questions about who we are and whether we can be trusted. No one wants to hire somebody who's likely to fly off in an unexpected direction every six months. So we downplay the very things that might make our stories compelling. To earn the listener's trust, we make ourselves appear safe—and dull and unremarkable.

Is there a way to tell a lively story *and* inspire others' confidence? Yes, but it requires a deep understanding of what really makes people believe in what we're saying.

The Struggle for Coherence

All good stories have a characteristic so basic and necessary it's often assumed. That quality is coherence, and it's crucial to life stories of transition.

This was a challenge for Sam Tierman, a former corporate HR executive one of us coached through a career transition. Sam had spent 18 years running HR in a number of good-sized regional banks, but his last three jobs hadn't ended well. He'd been downsized out of one, he'd quit another in frustration, and he'd been fired from the last—which finally led him to realize he had a career problem. While he was energized by the interplay between individuals and organizations, he hated the mundane, administrative aspects of the work. When he had a boss who considered HR a strategic function and who included the HR head at the executive table, he thrived. But when he worked for someone who saw HR as a body shop—"Find the bodies, run the benefits, and keep the government off our back"—Sam hated his work. In his last job, his feelings had been obvious, and a minor problem with some personnel analysis was what did him in. Sam, in fact, had taken this job with high hopes. The CEO who hired him considered HR strategic. Unfortunately, that CEO left and was replaced by one who did not.

As a result, Sam gave up on finding or keeping a boss he could work with in a corporate setting. As do so many frustrated executives, he decided he would prefer to work for a start-up. The problem was that he lacked, on the face of it, any of the experience or qualities wanted by people who found and fund start-ups. It was not obvious how Sam could tell a coherent career story that would bridge the chasm between stodgy overhead departments in banks and the high-energy world of start-ups.

Coherent narratives hang together in ways that feel natural and intuitive. A coherent life story is one that suggests what we all want to believe of ourselves and those we help or hire—that our lives are series of unfolding, linked events that make sense. In other words, the past is related to the present, and from that trajectory, we can glimpse our future.

Coherence is crucial to a life story of transition because it is the characteristic that most generates the listener's trust. If you can make your story of change and reinvention seem coherent, you will have gone far in convincing the listener that the change makes sense for you and is likely to bring success—and that you're a stable, trustworthy person.

As important, you will also have gone far in convincing yourself. Indeed, it's the loss of coherence that makes times of transition so difficult to get through. Think of the cartoon character who's run off the edge of a cliff.

Legs still churning like crazy, he doesn't realize he's over the abyss—until he looks down. Each of us in transition feels like that character. Coherence is the solid ground under our feet. Without it, we feel as though we're hanging in midair—and we're afraid that if we look down, we'll plummet to our doom.

Charlotte Linde, a linguist who has studied the importance of coherence in life stories, makes clear in her work that coherence emerges in large part from continuity and causality. If we fail to observe these two principles, we create a sense of incoherence, or, in Linde's words, the "chilling possibility that one's life is random, accidental, unmotivated." And what's chilling to us will certainly be off-putting to those listening to our stories.

Emphasizing Continuity and Causality

Now it becomes understandable why so many speakers in that networking meeting failed to do more than recite facts. They were trying to downplay discontinuity; to gloss over how large a professional jump they wanted to make; to avoid appearing wayward, lost, and flailing. It was a misguided strategy, for listeners are particularly sensitive to lapses of coherence in life stories. They actually *look for* coherence in such stories. Failure to acknowledge a large degree of change will put off listeners and undermine their trust.

As storytellers, we must deal explicitly with the magnitude of change our stories communicate. We can do that and still inspire trust if we focus on establishing continuity and causality. The following suggestions can help.

KEEP YOUR REASONS FOR CHANGE GROUNDED IN YOUR CHARACTER, IN WHO YOU ARE

There's probably no rationale for change more compelling than some internal reason, some basic character trait. In its simplest version, this explanation takes the form of "I discovered I'm good at that" or "I like that—it gives me real pleasure." This approach, noted by Linde and found by us in our work to be extremely useful, allows storytellers to incorporate learning and self-discovery into life stories. We can try something, learn from the experience, and use that learning to deepen our understanding of what we want. Many turning points can be used in this way. Note that it's not wise to base the reasons for transformation primarily outside ourselves. "I got fired" may be a fact we must explain and incorporate into our stories, but it's rarely recognized as a good justification for seeking whatever we're seeking. External reasons tend to create the impression that we simply accept our fate.

CITE MULTIPLE REASONS FOR WHAT YOU WANT

You might, for instance, mention both personal and professional grounds for making a change. (Obviously, these must be complementary rather than mutually exclusive or contradictory.) The richer and more varied the reasons compelling you to change, the more comprehensible and acceptable that change will appear. Sam, the former HR executive, was able to cite a number of unusual projects he had worked on, which indicated, though in a big-company context, his ability to think and act entrepreneurially. Additionally, his undergraduate training in electrical engineering and his MBA in finance from a prestigious school were evidence of the technical and analytical bent preferred by the start-ups he knew.

BE SURE TO POINT OUT ANY EXPLANATIONS THAT EXTEND BACK IN TIME

A goal rooted in the past will serve far better than one recently conceived. Your story will need to show why you could not pursue the goal originally, but here, external causes—illness, accident, family problems, being drafted, and so on—can play a leading role.

REFRAME YOUR PAST IN LIGHT OF THE CHANGE YOU RE SEEKING TO MAKE

This is not to suggest that you hide anything or prevaricate. We all continually rethink and retell our own life stories. We create different versions that focus on or downplay, include or exclude, different aspects of what has happened to us. Some elements of the jobs we've held probably fit well with our change plans and can be used to link our past experiences with the part of our life that we're advancing toward. The key is to dissect those experiences and find the pieces that relate to our current goals. (For advice on how to do this, see the insert "Does Your Résumé Tell a Story?" at the end of this article.)

CHOOSE A STORY FORM THAT LENDS ITSELF TO YOUR TALE OF REINVENTION

Certain forms—love stories, war stories, epics—are as old as narrative itself. There are stories of being tested and stories of being punished. When it comes to describing transition and reinvention, it can be helpful to present the story in a vessel familiar to most listeners. Of the time-honored approaches, two to consider are the maturation (or coming-of-age) plot and the education plot.

The maturation plot was useful to Gary McCarthy, who quit his job as a strategy consultant with no idea of what he would do next. As he told his story at age 35, he looked back over his career and realized he had always responded to social pressure, bending to what others thought was the right thing for him to do. After receiving a negative performance appraisal, he saw that he needed to be his own man. "You'd better be damn sure when you wake up that you're doing what you want to be doing," he said to himself, "as opposed to what you feel you ought to be doing or what somebody else thinks you ought to be doing."

Lucy Hartman's story is a good example of the education plot, which recounts change generated by growing insight and self-understanding. It was a mentor, her executive coach, who let her glimpse a possible new future, and she continued to learn in her master's program and by coaching others. In her version of events, the more she learned about the human side of enterprise, the more she realized her desire to work in and contribute to this area.

All these suggestions are ways to frame the discontinuity in a transition story and provide the coherence that will reassure listeners. They demonstrate that, at your core, the person you were yesterday is the person you are today and the person you will be tomorrow. And they establish that there are good and sufficient causes for change. If you create the sense that your life hangs (and will hang) together, you'll be free to incorporate the dramatic elements of change and turmoil and uncertainty into your story that will make it compelling.

Telling Multiple Stories

We've noted the challenge of crafting a story, complete with dramatic turning points, when the outcome is still far from clear. The truth is, as you embark on a career transition, you will likely find yourself torn among different interests, paths, and priorities. It wouldn't be unusual, for example, for you to work all weekend on a business plan for a start-up, return to your day job on Monday and ask for a transfer to another position or business unit, and then have lunch on Tuesday with a headhunter to explore yet a third option. This is simply the nature of career transition. So how do you reconcile this reality with the need to present a clear, single life story of reinvention, one that implies you know exactly where you're going?

For starters, keep in mind that, in a job interview, you don't establish trust by getting everything off your chest or being completely open about the several possibilities you are exploring. In the early stages of a transition, it is important to identify and actively consider multiple alternatives. But you will explore each option, or type of option, with a different audience.

This means that you must craft different stories for different possible selves (and the various audiences that relate to those selves). Sam chose to focus on start-ups as the result of a process that began with examining his own experience. He realized that he had felt most alive during times he described as "big change fast"—a bankruptcy, a turnaround, and a rapid reorganization. So he developed three stories to support his goal of building a work life around "big change fast": one about the HR contributions he could make on a team at a consulting company that specialized in taking clients through rapid change; one about working for a firm that bought troubled companies and rapidly turned them around; and one about working for a start-up, probably a venture between its first and second, or second and third, rounds of financing. He tested these stories on friends and at networking events and eventually wrangled referrals and job interviews for each kind of job.

The process is not only about keeping options open as long as possible; it's also about learning which ones to pursue most energetically. In Sam's case, what became clear over a number of conversations was that the consulting firms he respected tended not to hire people of his age and credentials unless they had perfectly relevant experience. Neither did opportunities with turnaround firms appear to be panning out. But Sam did make progress toward some start-ups. After one of them engaged him for a series of consulting assignments, he was able to convert that relationship into a job as chief administrative officer. That position, in turn, exposed him to many contacts in the start-up community. Most important, it stamped him as a bona fide member of that world. Having stripped the stodgy corporate aura from his résumé, he eventually became the CEO of a start-up set to commercialize some technology developed by and spun out of a large company. By this point, four full years had elapsed, and Sam had revised his narrative many times, with each step contributing to a more and more coherent story of change.

Just Tell It

Any veteran storyteller will agree that there's no substitute for practicing in front of a live audience. Tell and retell your story; rework it like a draft of an epic novel until the "right" version emerges.

You can practice your stories in many ways and places. Any context will do in which you're likely to be asked, "What can you tell me about yourself?" or "What do you do?" or "What are you looking for?" Start with family and friends. You may even want to designate a small circle of friends and close colleagues, with their knowledge and approval, your "board of advisers." Their primary function would be to listen and react again and again to your evolving stories. Many of the people we have studied or coached through the transition process have created or joined networking groups for just this purpose.

You'll know you've honed your story when it feels both comfortable and true to you. But you cannot get there until you put yourself in front of others— ultimately, in front of strangers—and watch their faces and body language as you speak. For one woman we know, June Prescott, it was not simply that practice made for polished presentation—although her early efforts to explain herself were provisional, even clumsy. (She was attempting a big career change, from academe to Wall Street.) Each time she wrote a cover letter, interviewed, or updated friends and family on her progress, she better defined what was exciting to her; and in each public declaration of her intent to change careers, she committed herself further.

June's experience teaches a final, important lesson about undergoing change. We use stories to reinvent ourselves. June, like Sam, was able to change because she created a story that justified and motivated such a dramatic shift.

This is the role of storytelling in times of personal transition. Getting the story right is critical, as much for motivating ourselves as for enlisting the help of others.

Anyone trying to make a change has to work out a story that connects the old and new selves. For it is in a period of change that we often fail, yet most need, to link our past, present, and future into a compelling whole.

Key Elements of a Classic Story

ALL GREAT STORIES, from *Antigone* to *Casablanca* to *Star Wars,* derive their power from several basic characteristics:

- **A protagonist the listener cares about.** The story must be about a person or group whose struggles we can relate to.

- **A catalyst compelling the protagonist to take action.** Somehow the world has changed so that something important is at stake. Typically, the first act of a play is devoted to establishing this fact. It's up to the protagonist to put things right again.

- **Trials and tribulations.** The story's second act commences as obstacles produce frustration, conflict, and drama, and often lead the protagonist to change in an essential way. As in *The Odyssey,* the trials reveal, test, and shape the protagonist's character. Time is spent wandering in the wilderness, far from home.

- **A turning point.** This represents a point of no return, which closes the second act. The protagonist can no longer see or do things the same way as before.

- **A resolution.** This is the third act, in which the protagonist either succeeds magnificently or fails tragically.

This is the classic beginning-middle-end story structure defined by Aristotle more than 2,300 years ago and used by countless others since. It seems to reflect how the human mind wants to organize reality.

Does Your Résumé Tell a Story?

THOUGH THE TERMS ARE often used interchangeably, there's a big difference between a curriculum vitae and a résumé.

A CV is an exhaustive and strictly chronological list of facts about your professional life. You may need one, but don't expect it to serve your cause in a period of transition. To the extent it tells a story, that story is constructed wholly in the reader's mind.

If you want to give your credentials narrative shape, use a résumé—and understand that you will almost certainly need more than one version. Each will highlight and interpret your experience differently in light of the job or career alternatives you're exploring.

The process of putting together a résumé is as valuable as the product, because it entails drafting your story. Everything in the résumé must point to one goal—which, of course, is the climax of the story you're telling. Build it in three parts.

First, describe the position you want.

Second, create a bulleted list of experience highlights that clearly demonstrate your ability to do that job. Consider every piece of experience you have (don't forget volunteer work or anything else that might apply), and identify which parts support the story you're telling.

Third, summarize your professional work. This section of your résumé has the appearance of a CV, in reverse chronological order, and includes all the relevant positions you've held; for each job, it shows dates of employment as well as your responsibilities and accomplishments. But these descriptions are couched in the same terms as your experience highlights. In fact, every claim in your highlights section (which supports your overall goal) must be supported by your job summaries.

Follow these steps, and your résumé will tell a coherent story. The work you have done, and the skills and interests you have developed and revealed, will point to a clear and desirable resolution: your stated goal.

Originally published in January 2005
Reprint R0501F

About the Contributors

JANET BANKS is a former managing director at FleetBoston Financial and a former vice president at Chase Manhattan Bank, responsible for leadership development and succession planning. She lives in Boston and continues to facilitation work for nonprofits.

DIANE COUTU was a communications specialist at McKinsey & Company and an affiliate scholar and Julius Silberger fellow at the Boston Psychoanalytic Society and Institute. She is currently a senior editor at HBR and a 2008-09 fellow at the American Psychiatric Institute.

RONALD A. HEIFETZ and MARTY LINSKY teach leadership at the John F. Kennedy School of Government at Harvard. They are partners of Cambridge Leadership Associates, a firm that consults to senior executives on the practice of leadership. They are also coauthors of *Leadership on the Line: Staying Alive Through the Dangers of Leading* Harvard Business Press, from which this article is adapted.

HERMINIA IBARRA is the Insead Chaired Professor of Organizational Behavior at Insead in Fontainebleau, France, and the author of *Working Identity: Unconventional Strategies for Reinventing Your Career* Harvard Business School Press, 2003.

KENT LINEBACK is a Cambridge, Massachusetts-based writer and coach on storytelling and change.

MARYANNE PEABODY and **LAURENCE J. STYBEL** are the founding partners of Stybel Peabody Lincolnshire, a Boston-based consulting firm.

KATHLEEN K. REARDON is a professor of management and organization at the University of Southern California Marshall School of Business.

JEFFERY A. SONNENFELD is a senior associate dean for executive programs, the Lester Crown Professor of Management Practice at the Yale School of Management, and the president of the Executive Leadership Institute at Yale University in New Haven, Connecticut.

ANDREW J. WARD is an assistant professor of management at the University of Georgia in Athens, Georgia. This article is drawn from their book of the same title from Harvard Business Press.

Index